To

From

Date

Miracle
IN THE
Making

THE DEVOTIONAL FOR
Expectant Moms

Miracle in the Making: The Devotional for Expectant Moms
Copyright © 2023 DaySpring. All rights reserved.
First Edition, May 2023

Published by:

21154 Highway 16 East
Siloam Springs, AR 72761
dayspring.com

All rights reserved. *Miracle in the Making: The Devotional for Expectant Moms* is under copyright protection. No part of this book may be used or reproduced in any manner whatsoever without written permission except in the case of brief quotations embodied in critical articles and reviews.

Scripture quotations marked ESV are taken from the ESV Bible® (The Holy Bible, English Standard Version®) copyright ©2001 by Crossway Bibles, a publishing ministry of Good News Publishers. Used by permission. All rights reserved.

Scripture quotations marked CSB® are taken from the Christian Standard Bible®, Copyright © 2017 by Holman Bible Publishers. Used by permission. Christian Standard Bible®, and CSB® are federally registered trademarks of Holman Bible Publishers.

Scripture quotations marked NASB are taken from the NEW AMERICAN STANDARD BIBLE ®, © Copyright 1960, 1962, 1963, 1968, 1971, 1972, 1973, 1975, 1977, 1995 by the Lockman Foundation. Used by permission. (www.lockman.org)

Scripture quotations marked NLT are taken from the Holy Bible, New Living Translation, copyright © 1996, 2004, 2007 by Tyndale House Foundation. Used by permission of Tyndale House Publishers, Inc., Carol Stream, Illinois 60188. All rights reserved.

Written by: Kristin Cortner
Cover Design by: Becca Barnett

Printed in India
Prime: J9591
ISBN: 978-1-64870-916-6

Contents

Introduction 9

Section 1: Learning to Trust

A Testing in Trust 10

When Fear Comes to Drown 12

Surrounded by Supporters 14

Wisdom for Uncertainty 16

Leaning on God's Timing 18

Our Part in God's Story 20

Peace Like a River 22

Section 2: Encouragement and Joy

In the Footsteps of Mary 24

Flutters and Kicks 26

Climbing the Mountain Through Milestones . 28

God's Very Present Help 30

Sitting with Anticipation 32

Learning from a Perfect Parent 34

Supplying for Needs 36

Section 3: Sacrificial Love

Perseverance from Paul 38

Emotions Like an Ocean 40

Strength for Today 42

Smiling Through the Pain 44
Learning from Jesus' Sacrifice 46
Laboring for Your Child 48
What Is True Love? 50

Section 4: Focusing Your Mind
The Dichotomy of Pregnancy Emotions 52
Savoring Moments 54
The Strongest Defense 56
The Great Wait 58
Centering Your Thoughts 60
Holding on to Contentment 62

Section 5: Changing Perspectives
Balancing Busyness 64
Straight from the Garden 66
Raising a Child in Today's World 68
The True Creator of Life 70
Cutting Down on Complaining 72
Embracing Seasons 74
A Daily Dose of Gratitude 76

Section 6: Giving Grace
Leaning on Your Husband 78
Let the Tears Fall 80
Learning to Forgive 82
Comparison and Bitterness 84

Embracing Your New Body 86
Treating Yourself with Kindness 88
A Routine of Rest 90

Section 7: Becoming More Like Jesus

Leading from Ahead 92
An Attitude of Service 94
Living Out Our Mission 96
Walking Authentically 98
Holding Tight to His Word 100
Washing Feet. 102
Maintaining Obedience 104

Section 8: The Walk of Surrender

Surrendering Your Child. 106
Surrendering Your Own Plans 108
A Lesson from Hannah. 110
A Lesson from Abraham 112
God's Ways Are Not Our Ways 114
Surrendering Our Own Strength. 116
Surrendering the Past 118

Section 9: Praying for Your Baby

Praying for Your Baby's Faith. 120
Praying for Your Baby's Birth 122
Praying for Your Baby's Health 124
Praying for Your Baby's Character. 126

    Praying for Your Baby's Childhood 128
    Praying for Your Baby's Future Friends 130
    Praying for Your Baby's Future Spouse 132

Section 10: Preparation Journey

    Preparing Your Heart 134

    Preparing a Special Place 136

    Preparing to Love 138

    Preparing Financially 140

    Preparing Your Family 142

    Preparing a Faith Foundation 144

    A Lesson from Deborah 146

Section 11: The Call to Motherhood

    The Miracle of Pregnancy 148

    Making Disciples 150

    What It Means to Be Mama 152

    The Role of Caretaker 154

    A Lifelong Commitment 156

    For Such a Time As This 158

Introduction

Pregnancy is a time of expectation, waiting, challenges, discomfort, and miracles. It's a season of preparation while you're growing a sweet little life inside. It's an amazing and miraculous time. And the real truth? It's incredibly difficult. This devotional will invite you into a walk of encouragement as you journey through the months of pregnancy. It includes stories about biblical women who exhibit strength and character and Scripture that will inspire you. Hopefully, you'll laugh and cry through these pages as you wait for your new baby to join you.

Pregnancy can bring up fears and failures, but it can also be a time when we challenge ourselves to rely on God like never before for the strength to endure. You're not alone. I had the joy of writing the majority of these devotionals while I was pregnant with our son. I hope you'll experience companionship and confidence in these pages. My pregnancy was a roller coaster of emotions. I wept in pain and discomfort. I paced endlessly at all hours of the night. And I filled journals with prayers and fears about my baby's future. But God created the miracle of pregnancy for a special reason. He chose *you* to be a mommy right now. Pregnancy will remind you that you're not in control. God can be the strength you need in this season. There is an amazing, miraculous thing happening right now inside of your body. And in the end? You'll realize just how thankful you were for it all.

A Testing in Trust

> And those who know your name
> put their trust in you,
> for you, O Lord, have not forsaken
> those who seek you.
>
> PSALM 9:10 ESV

Whether you are expecting your fourth child or you've just found out that you're pregnant with your very first baby, pregnancy is a time of testing. There is so much beauty in creating a little life inside your own body. It's a privilege. But it's also a time when life feels so out of control. And who doesn't like to feel in control? We make our routines. We make our plans, and we follow all the rules in an effort to feel like we are in charge of our lives. But pregnancy is something that is really out of our hands. We can follow every piece of advice our doctor gives us, and sometimes bad things still happen. Sometimes we still find ourselves fraught with worry and anxiety (especially during the first trimester). What will happen to this little budding life? Will he or she make it to the second trimester? What will we do if something happens?

When these concerns, worries, and thoughts enter our heads, it's best to turn to God's Word. The truth is, we could hold on with tight fists and spend weeks fretting over things we have very little control over, or we could let go and choose to trust the scheme of God's plans.

Pregnancy is a true test of our trust in God. His plans may not always make sense to us, but He is trustworthy. Whatever comes your way, God is faithful. Faithful to walk by your side in good times and bad. Faithful to grant you peace and provide whatever you need each and every day. He knows you, and He knows your baby intimately. You can put your own health and your baby's life and growth in His hands. He is capable of holding all your worries and fears. Choose to trust Him today. He will never forsake those who seek Him.

Lord,
though I am scared sometimes for myself and my child,
I choose today to leave my fears with You and trust You.
You are in control. You will not forsake me,
no matter what may come my way.
Amen.

When Fear Comes to Drown

*When the cares of my heart are many,
your consolations cheer my soul.*
PSALM 94:19 ESV

Fear can feel like a tangible, living monster that is coiled inside of us, ready to devour us whole. It can seem overwhelming and stifling, blocking our view of the future and stealing away all the joyful moments and thoughts that we might have about pregnancy. It's normal to feel afraid when you're carrying something so precious inside. Your child is so small and vulnerable in these months growing in the womb. You might be afraid of losing that little life. Or maybe you're struggling with an overwhelming fear of the future and what it looks like to be a mom. Perhaps you feel afraid of the months of pregnancy to come and whatever hardships could be in store. Each woman will carry different fears unique to her, but all fear can become an overwhelming burden.

Read the story in Matthew 14:22–33. Peter was afraid when he stepped onto those waves, and he allowed his fear to overwhelm him and drag him down into the depths of the lake. He put his attention on his fears rather than on his Savior, Jesus, who was with him in the midst of the storm the entire time. When Peter shouted, "Lord, save me!" Jesus was there in an instant with a hand outstretched to pull him from the waves of his fear.

This story is a reminder that, sometimes, God calls us into a rocky place where we don't feel in control. Pregnancy can feel like a rocking boat in the middle of the storm. But Jesus is always there with us. He's with you right now, offering an outstretched hand when you feel like you're drowning in fear. Keep your eyes on Jesus and allow His peace and presence to console those fears within you.

Lord,

the fears are rising up against me,
and it makes me feel like I'm drowning.
Help me keep my eyes on You today and
off the things I cannot control.
Thank You for promising to be with me in the storms.

Amen.

Surrounded by Supporters

*For if either falls, his companion can lift him up;
but pity the one who falls without another to lift him up.
Also, if two lie down together, they can keep warm;
but how can one person alone keep warm?
And if someone overpowers one person, two can resist
him. A cord of three strands is not easily broken.*
ECCLESIASTES 4:10–12 CSB

Have you felt isolated during pregnancy? Especially during the first trimester, you might be keeping your pregnancy a secret from family and friends until you reach twelve weeks or more. This can make you feel lonely and unseen as you struggle through those difficult first few weeks. Throughout the entire pregnancy, you could have plenty of well-wishers asking you how you're feeling and if you're excited and how far along you are. While the masses of people have best wishes for you and your baby, they probably don't know exactly what you're feeling on the inside. This can become even more isolating if you feel like you're holding in your discomfort, anxiety, or frustration.

But you don't have to walk through this season on your own. First and foremost, God is by your side, and He is not afraid of your honesty, however brutal. In addition, what people in your life can you surround yourself with during these months? Look for individuals who are encouraging and supportive. Find a mom you admire who is in the next stage of life and ask her to be a supportive mentor during your pregnancy. Gather together close, trustworthy friends and family members who will walk through this journey with you and ask them to commit to pray for you, your baby, and the other members of your family.

We don't have to walk through life alone. God's vision for His people is to be a strong, supportive community for one another. You can lean on your friends in these hard times and ask people to be praying for you. Don't be afraid to be honest about how you're feeling. Other moms can understand and offer encouragement. And someday, maybe you'll be that voice of encouragement for another expectant mom.

Lord,

thank You for creating us to be in community with other people. Bring individuals into my life who can be an encouragement and a prayer support for me during my pregnancy. Thank You that I don't have to walk this path alone.

Amen.

Wisdom for Uncertainty

> If any of you lacks wisdom, let him ask God,
> who gives generously to all without reproach,
> and it will be given him.
> **JAMES 1:5 ESV**

Decisions, decisions, decisions. From the moment a woman stares at that "positive" sign on a pregnancy test to the moment she finally gets to hold her baby in her arms, she's presented with a plethora of choices and decisions to make. Some are relatively small choices, like what brand of prenatal vitamin she wants. But others are significant. What hospital will she choose? Does she want a home birth or a hospital delivery? Epidural or natural? And of course, what will the baby's name be? Does she want to know the gender ahead of time? Where will the baby go to day care? The list can grow in length as the pregnancy progresses and she gets closer and closer to her due date. The significance of each choice can feel heavy and the decisions hard to make. What should she do?

Thankfully, we have a God who promises to give wisdom to those who seek it out. God will give wisdom generously without making you feel ashamed for asking. He never wants you to hold back from asking Him for help for any decision, big or small. He's right there, ready and waiting to help you, if only you would ask.

When the next big choice comes during your pregnancy, take a pause and go to the Lord to ask for wisdom about what you should do. There may be people who can give you counsel, but ultimately, you can make your own decisions with the wisdom that God is so generously willing to provide His children. You can do this. One step at a time.

Lord God,

thank You for promising to give wisdom generously when I ask. I do need wisdom. I can't make these big decisions on my own. Please show me the direction and the path You want me to take during my pregnancy.

Amen.

Leaning on God's Timing

Trust in the Lord with all your heart, and do not lean on your own understanding. In all your ways acknowledge him, and he will make straight your paths.
PROVERBS 3:5–6 ESV

Have you ever felt like you were waiting for something for an eternity? Have you ever wondered if God was simply not listening to a prayer coming from the depths of your soul? For many expectant mothers, you've been waiting for and praying for this specific season to come. Perhaps you and your husband spent years trying to get pregnant. Through fertility treatments, doctors' visits, disappointing months, and countless prayers, maybe you thought that God would never show up. But now He has! Or, on the other hand, perhaps this pregnancy was unexpected in your own plans and timing. Maybe you had a big shock when you found out you were pregnant. Why did God choose now? Why couldn't He have waited just a little longer, to when you might have felt more ready? Whatever your pregnancy story has been, God has chosen now. Right now. We may not understand His ways and His purposes, but His timing is always best.

Our part in His timing is to simply accept it and to trust in His plans. For creatures who like the illusion of control, this is hard to do. Pregnancy will illuminate our lack of control more than many other seasons in our lives. We can't control the timing of our pregnancy. God is the One who creates life, not us. We can't control when the baby comes or if he or she will be premature or right on time. But we can put our trust in the Lord with all of our heart and learn to lean on His understanding, not ours. That might mean that your pregnancy journey looks different than you imagined, but God has a plan in mind. You can lean into Him.

God,

thank You that You've chosen this season in my life to bring this little life into the world. You've known all along that this timing would be best. I trust in Your big plan for my life and for the life of my baby.

Amen.

Our Part in God's Story

> The counsel of the LORD stands forever,
> the plans of His heart from generation to generation.
> **PSALM 33:11 CSB**

Take a few moments and step back from your current situation, the pregnancy symptoms, the fears and worries . . . everything. Focus instead on the timeline of humanity. Mankind has existed for a long time. The Bible tells the story of humans from creation to the end of everything in the book of Revelation. Billions of people live and die each day, and God sees and knows them all. Through the chaos of the Old Testament to the coming of Jesus Christ in the New Testament, there is a beautiful narrative of hope, redemption, and purpose. It's God's story, playing out in His creation and revealing His plans through us. Doesn't it make you feel small in comparison to the vastness of God and His big story? Millions of women will give birth this year, and God knows each and every new life that comes into this world.

While it can feel overwhelming in scope, it's also comforting to know that we have a specific part to play in God's story. He invites us into His plans for humanity. Above all, He desires relationship with us; He wants that with you and, someday, with your child. There has been a plan from the very beginning, and there will still be a plan long after we leave this world. God is so big and vast when compared to our daily aches, pains, and nausea. But He cares! Instead of reigning above His creation in the Garden of Eden, God chose to come down and walk amongst the trees with Adam and Eve because He wanted to know them. We each have a role to play in God's story. The child you are carrying also has a role to play. It's an honor to be invited into the vast, redemptive story that God is carrying out!

Almighty God,

You are so vast and big compared to us, but You want us to know You. You invite us into this redemption story that You have been weaving together since the beginning. Help me to truly comprehend the role that I get to play in that story by bringing this baby into the world.

Amen.

Miracle in the Making

Peace Like a River

> "Peace I leave with you. My peace I give to you.
> I do not give to you as the world gives.
> Don't let your heart be troubled or fearful."
> JOHN 14:27 CSB

The hymn, "It Is Well with My Soul," is a beautiful song of surrender and trust, and it still brings peace and comfort to many people today. However, lyrics that have offered hope to many were penned under intense grief and tragedy. Horatio Spafford and his wife had one son and four daughters in 1871, and Spafford had a successful law and real estate business in Chicago. That year, they tragically lost their son to scarlet fever and their fortune to the Great Chicago Fire. Reeling with loss, the family limped on until 1873. Spafford sent his wife and four daughters on a sea voyage across the Atlantic Ocean to Europe, where he planned to meet them for a vacation later on. During the journey, the ship struck another vessel and sank. Panic and desperation must have been overwhelming for Spafford as he waited for word of his family. Finally, he received a short telegram from his wife.

"Saved alone."

Spafford boarded a ship soon after to meet his wife so they could grieve together. As his ship passed over the very waters where his remaining children had perished, he felt inspired and compelled to pen the words to the hymn that we still sing today. The lyrics take on a new light when we read his story: "When peace like a river attendeth my way, when sorrows like sea billows roll; whatever my lot, Thou hast taught me to say, it is well, it is well with my soul." We can feel very wrapped up in our own stories and struggles. It's not easy to declare that "it is well with my soul" when things feel very, very unwell. It takes amazing faith and trust to say, "whatever my lot, I will still remain at peace because of what God has done for me." Sometimes peace is a declaration and a choice, despite how we feel. Sometimes it's a desperate cry of "it is well with my soul."

Jesus,
thank You for granting me peace that dwells
in my heart. Thank You that You're with me
in the storms of life. I can confidently say
"it is well with my soul," because You are with me.
Amen.

In the Footsteps of Mary

And Mary said, "My soul magnifies the Lord, and my spirit rejoices in God my Savior, for he has looked on the humble estate of his servant. For behold, from now on all generations will call me blessed; for he who is mighty has done great things for me, and holy is his name."
LUKE 1:46–49 ESV

Mary, the mother of Jesus, was truly a remarkable woman. She was very young when she conceived Jesus by the Holy Spirit, probably in her mid-teenage years. And yet, her faith was amazing. When the angel Gabriel told her that she would have a son, she answered, "May it be done to me according to your word" (Luke 1:38 NASB). She was probably scared. Childbirth in her time was dangerous without the modern medicine we have today. Not only that, but she was walking into a difficult nine months knowing that she could be scorned and ostracized by her community for becoming pregnant before marriage. Can you just imagine the thoughts and fears running through her mind about the days ahead? Can you relate? Even when we want to get pregnant, when we find out for the first time that we are indeed having a baby, our thoughts can go from excited to shocked to terrified in a matter of minutes.

But Mary's faith in her Lord was deep. She knew that He was in control and had a plan. So she responded in obedience, faithfully walking forward into whatever would come her way. During that time period, she could have been stoned to death for becoming pregnant before marriage. But read today's verse again. She says that her "spirit rejoices in God my Savior." What a beautiful proclamation of trust and acceptance. She might not have thought that she was ready to be a mother, especially not to the promised Messiah, but she praised the Lord for all the good things He had already done and was going to do! We can follow in Mary's footsteps. Through all of pregnancy's aches and pains and discomfort, we can still remember to give our praise back to God. Because what a beautiful, good thing He is doing through it all.

Lord,

just as Mary proclaimed her love and devotion to You through her song, I also give You praise for what You are doing in my body and in the life of my growing baby. Thank You for choosing me to carry this burden. I am Your humble servant.

Amen.

Flutters and Kicks

*Every good and perfect gift is from above,
coming down from the Father of lights,
who does not change like shifting shadows.*
JAMES 1:17 CSB

At around twenty-four weeks' pregnant, you may start to experience an odd sensation in the pit of your belly. It may feel like a small bubble or a bit of stomach digestion. You might pause, cock your head, and wonder if that little movement could be something . . . more. Or you might shake your head and continue on with your day. But as your pregnancy progresses, those little tiny bubbles of movements and flutters will grow stronger and stronger until there is no denying the reality. There is a small, but distinct, living being inside your body, and he or she is already moving on their own, showing their independence and desire for life. The moment you feel your child kicking in the womb, your pregnancy will feel completely and entirely real. After the initial shock and surprise wears off when the baby moves, you'll start looking forward to those secret moments. It's a special experience between a mother and her baby. One that only you can have.

God designed pregnancy in this way to give mothers

those secret moments of bonding before anyone else can feel those flutters and kicks. Once the kicks strengthen to the point that others can feel them, the magic of the moment is then shared with others. Savor each flutter and kick. When you feel those tiny little hands and feet stretching and extending, say a prayer of thanks that your baby is healthy and growing. There really is a small, beautiful human being growing and developing right inside of the body that God created for you. In the midst of the struggles, aches, and stresses that pregnancy can bring about, there are those quiet, still moments between you, God, and your baby that you can remember and cherish. Your baby is such a gift from the Lord. Use each and every kick (even when they start to hurt) to thank the Lord for the life that He is creating with your help.

Jesus,

thank You that every good and perfect gift comes from You.
My baby is a beautiful gift.
Thank You for reminding me of how precious
each and every moment is, from one kick to the next.

Amen.

Climbing the Mountain Through Milestones

> Brothers and sisters, I do not consider myself
> to have taken hold of it. But one thing I do:
> Forgetting what is behind and reaching forward
> to what is ahead, I pursue as my goal the prize promised
> by God's heavenly call in Christ Jesus.
>
> PHILIPPIANS 3:13–14 CSB

Do you ever feel like pregnancy is like running a marathon? When you first start off, you look at the miles and miles waiting ahead of you. You gaze at the uphill climbs and the harrowing descents and the long stretches of open road that seem endless. Many marathon runners will say that they never focus on the length of the race itself or how far they've gone. Instead, they only focus on the next milestone, the next refuel station, the next goal.

It's easy to get overwhelmed by the remaining weeks of your pregnancy. Time can feel like it's slowing down or going backward. Instead, focus your mind on the next milestone ahead, and ask God to grant you the strength to make it there. If you're in your first trimester, your next big milestone might be hitting twelve weeks' pregnant, when you can share your news with friends and family.

Or perhaps your next milestone is your twenty-week ultrasound, when you'll be able to see your baby for the first time. Or maybe it's getting to the third and final trimester, when you have a baby shower or take your labor and delivery class.

Live each day in the present, but set your mind on what is coming next. This pregnancy is only one small length of time in the scope of your life. Your lifetime goal should be to run toward Christ with all your heart, just like you're running a race as if to win the gold medal. You can run this race of pregnancy. What an amazing prize you have at the end of it, when you finally get to hold your baby in your arms.

Lord,
help me to keep climbing this mountain step by step.
Thank You for being with me through
each and every milestone. I want to keep
running toward You with all my heart
so I can teach my child how to
journey after You as well.
Amen.

God's Very Present Help

God is our refuge and strength,
a very present help in trouble.
Therefore we will not fear though the earth gives way.
PSALM 46:1–2 ESV

The psalmist in Psalm 46:2 has it right when he states that the "earth gives way." One glance at the news can cause a rush of anxiety to take over. One look at our bank account can make us feel wholly inadequate and unprepared for the future. One moment of reflection can have us doubting whether we have the strength to walk this path of motherhood and pregnancy at all. How can we bring a new life into this chaos? How can we find the money to pay our medical bills? How can we walk forward in confidence when we're overcome with fear of the future?

Psalm 46:1 starts with a message of hope and comfort: "God is our refuge and strength, a very present help in trouble." The words "very present help" are powerful. God is not just present in our world. He doesn't just preside high and above the chaos beneath. He's very present in our specific circumstances and in our personal lives. While we can never fully understand why bad things happen or why it feels like we are always the underdog in our individual situations, we aren't alone.

We can look at God as a "refuge" and our "strength." The Hebrew word for "refuge" is *machaseh*, which means "a shelter." King David and the other psalmists often use this word in correlation with words like "stronghold," "fortress," or "strong tower." It's a place of safety, but it's also a place of trust and protection. God is our safe place—our protection when the world feels like it's simply falling apart. He is very present with us today. Take hold of that truth and let it strengthen you with courage and comfort.

Lord God,

I need Your refuge and strength today. Thank You for promising to be a very present help in trouble. I'm not alone, for You are with me through it all. Thank You that I don't have to fear when I'm sheltered in Your safe presence.

Amen.

Sitting with Anticipation

*And not only the creation, but we ourselves,
who have the firstfruits of the Spirit,
groan inwardly as we wait eagerly for adoption as sons,
the redemption of our bodies.*

ROMANS 8:23 ESV

Merriam-Webster's dictionary describes the word *anticipation* as "the act of looking forward." It's generally used in a positive instance or as a pleasurable expectation. Think of a child on Christmas Eve, eagerly awaiting the magic of Christmas morning, when they can wake up to the smells of a warm breakfast and the promise of new gifts waiting to be ripped open. The days leading up to a wedding are filled with excitement and impatient anticipation to finally be united as husband and wife before God and our friends and family. Sometimes, in pregnancy, we can forget to be filled with eager anticipation of the coming of new life. We can get so caught up in the daily trials, fatigue, and pain that we forget to be excited! This season will end, sooner than you think, and you'll be able to see and touch and smell this incredible miracle who's been growing all this time.

Paul writes in Romans 8:23 that creation and the Church should "groan inwardly as we wait eagerly" for

God to finish His work of redemption. Because one day, creation will be free of its bondage of sin, and we will be made new in heaven with Jesus. New bodies, new creation, complete redemption. What a promise that we can look forward to! Just like a child on Christmas Eve, we can sit with great anticipation as we wait for Jesus to come back and complete His work. Just like those hectic, joy-filled days before our wedding, we can eagerly await the fulfillment of God's promise to make everything new on this earth.

But for today, let yourself feel that pleasurable expectation and excitement that comes with being a mother to a new child. The road ahead is long and will have challenges, but you can still look forward to the amazing gift of seeing your baby for the first time. One day, just around the corner, you'll get to look him or her in the eyes and know that the waiting was worth it.

Jesus,

I do eagerly await Your coming and the fulfillment of Your promise to make this world new. Help me to likewise anticipate the arrival of my child in the coming months. Help me to sit with anticipation with both patience and great excitement.

Amen.

Learning from a Perfect Parent

> Love the LORD your God with all your heart,
> with all your soul, and with all your strength.
> These words that I am giving you today are to be
> in your heart. Repeat them to your children. Talk about
> them when you sit in your house and when you walk
> along the road, when you lie down and when you get up.
> **DEUTERONOMY 6:5–7 CSB**

Am I going to be a good mom? Most likely, this thought has flitted through your mind in the first few months of pregnancy. Even if this is not your first child, you might remember worrying about this very question. A slew of other questions can overtake you from there: *How can I raise godly children? How will I discipline? What if I don't know what to do? What if I'm not enough?*

These are common fears, and parents have been asking these questions for centuries. God gave His chosen people, the Israelites, some parenting instructions in the book of Deuteronomy. His first step toward godly parenting is for parents to get their hearts right before Him. Prioritizing our own walk of faith before anything else is key.

What a privilege it is for us to have access to the

entire Bible. The Israelites only had half the story. We have the full, completed manuscript of God's redemption story. God's advice? Dig deep into His Word until the text is engraved in our hearts and minds.

Then God, the only perfect parent to ever exist, teaches us how to raise our children. We don't have to worry about being a good parent. God is a good Father, and He is our model and our guide. So the next time those fearful thoughts come in, rest in assurance that you can learn from the one and only perfect Parent.

Dear God,

thank You for being a good Father to Your children. Thank You for teaching me how to raise my children and for promising to help me along the journey. I'm still afraid of the future, but I know that You'll be there to guide me through.

Amen.

Supplying for Needs

*And my God will supply all your needs
according to His riches in glory in Christ Jesus.*
PHILIPPIANS 4:19 csb

Pregnancy can bring about acute stress and anxiety for many, many reasons. Your body is changing. Your strength is flagging. Your hormones are setting off various moods and emotions that are hard to rein in. There is a lot to plan for and many things to do. Very few moms will feel completely and totally prepared for having a child. It's perfectly normal to feel a bit overwhelmed by the new reality coming your way. Medical bills can start to roll in from your prenatal appointments and ultrasounds. You are probably trying to find a way to purchase a car seat, a crib, diapers, and many other baby essentials. In a time of joy and expectation, it might feel like you and your husband are drowning in bills and expenses that you weren't ready for. The burden of financial strain could be overshadowing the blessing that pregnancy is meant to be.

Does the Bible say that you will never experience financial stress? No. In fact, many of the early Christians lived in great poverty. In Philippians 4, Paul thanks the church in Philippi for generously giving to his ministry, even in the midst of their own financial need. They modeled trusting God with their finances and needs, and they continued to walk in generous obedience. You might recognize Philippians 4:19: "And my God will supply all your needs according to His riches in glory in Christ Jesus." Is Paul stating that you will never experience hardship or need? No. The church in Philippi still had strain, but God did provide for their needs. It may not look exactly how you imagine. The baby's nursery may not have all the bells and whistles you want. It may take time to pay off medical bills. You may have to crunch your budget to incorporate caring for a new baby. But God does show up to help in His way and in His timing. He loves to use His own people to do this, as seen from the Philippian church. So when someone offers you hand-me-down clothes or baby furniture, thank the Lord for using His people in your life!

Jesus,

thank You for teaching us how to be generous with our finances, even when it feels like we are the ones in need. Thank You for providing in the small things and in the big things. Please help us prepare for our child financially. We choose to trust You with our needs.

Amen.

Perseverance from Paul

If I must boast, I would rather boast about the things that show how weak I am.
II CORINTHIANS 11:30 NLT

The apostle Paul knew and understood pain and suffering. In fact, he suffered tremendously for his faith after he became a Christian. His entire life became one of traveling endlessly, facing persecution and torture, and working hard to keep the early churches on the right path. In II Corinthians 11, Paul lists the trials that he'd faced for his faith. The list includes prison, flogging, beatings, three shipwrecks, a night adrift at sea, hunger, thirst, sleepless nights, and freezing temperatures (read II Corinthians 11:16–33 and 12:1–10). It's truly terrible what Paul endured in his lifetime, but he never let it stop him from persevering. He kept going forward no matter what trials he faced. He writes in II Corinthians 12:10 (NLT): "That's why I take pleasure in my weaknesses, and in the insults, hardships, persecutions, and troubles that I suffer for Christ. For when I am weak, then I am strong." What a testament to his faith in Jesus Christ!

Most likely, we will not face what Paul faced in his lifetime. We probably won't be flogged or thrown in prison. Hopefully, we won't live through three shipwrecks or spend a night alone in the middle of the ocean. But we will experience trials. Pregnancy might be that for you. Perhaps you feel at the end of your rope today. Perhaps the road ahead feels too long and too painful to face. Our bodies endure quite a lot during pregnancy and birth. It's okay to admit that we don't feel well, that we're tired, and that we're struggling. But we can also follow Paul's example in the midst of our circumstances. He never gave up, though most people would have quit. He told the church in Corinth that his weaknesses made him stronger because they required him to rely on God for enduring strength. Again and again, God showed up for Paul. He will show up for you.

Jesus,
I feel like I'm in the midst of a trial in my life.
It feels like I can't keep going. I do feel weak.
But I know that even in my weakness,
You can make me strong. Please help me persevere.
Amen.

Emotions Like an Ocean

> I waited patiently for the LORD, and He turned to me and heard my cry for help. He brought me up from a desolate pit, out of the muddy clay, and set my feet on a rock, making my steps secure.
> **PSALM 40:1–2 CSB**

Growing a baby is hard work. It can do funny things to your body. And it can do far more to your emotions. In the first trimester, your emotions can be all over the place. One day, you'll feel okay. The next, you might feel like you're drowning in depression. You might cry about the silliest things, or sometimes, for absolutely no reason at all. There may be mornings when your mood will feel so heavy that you don't feel like you can get out of bed to start the day. Throughout your entire pregnancy, your emotions may flex and change, like an ocean. One moment, you'll be calm and focused, like gentle waves on a gorgeous, sunny beach. The next, you may feel like a raging hurricane of frustration. You may even start asking, "Am I going crazy, God? Will I ever feel like myself again?"

If you've asked the same questions, take heart. You're not going crazy. Pregnancy affects your hormones, and everyone reacts differently. Some women may not experience emotional turmoil during pregnancy. Other women can feel like an ever-changing ocean of emotions that no meteorologist can predict. There are moments of real despair and desolation.

King David wrote most of the book of Psalms. Throughout the pages, you'll see him crying out for help with gut-wrenching honesty. He was not afraid of his dark emotions. But he went to God for comfort. The next time you feel like you're gazing up from a "desolate pit," call on God for emotional strength. He, more than anyone else, understands exactly how you feel.

Lord God,

I feel like I'm standing on unsteady ground. My emotions are hard to control. I don't feel like myself. Please turn to me and comfort me today. Help me to give myself grace and to walk forward in confidence.

Amen.

Strength for Today

"Do not fear, for I am with you; do not be afraid, for I am your God. I will strengthen you; I will help you; I will hold on to you with My righteous right hand."

ISAIAH 41:10 CSB

One of the most beloved hymns by Christians today is "Great Is Thy Faithfulness." The hymn began as a poem, penned by a poet named Thomas Chisholm and eventually set to music by William Runyan in 1923. Billy Graham made the hymn popular by playing it during his worldwide crusades, and today, it's sung in church services, funerals, and weddings as a reminder of God's enduring faithfulness to each one of us. Have you ever stopped to ponder the beautiful lyrics of the hymn? Verse 3 of the song has an applicable message for this season of your life: "Pardon for sin and a peace that endureth; Thine own dear presence to cheer and to guide; strength for today and bright hope for tomorrow; blessings all mine with ten thousand beside." Take a moment to soak in those words: "strength for today and bright hope for tomorrow." You don't have to conquer your entire pregnancy at once. What you need from God is strength to get through *today*.

Isaiah 41:10 is an encouraging message from God to His people, the Israelites, who were in captivity in Babylon. He gently reminds them that He is with them. They do not have to be afraid. And neither do you. God will strengthen you today. He will help you. He will hold tightly to you as you walk along this journey. Don't focus on the days ahead. Instead, thank the Lord for the new day. Ask Him to grant you the strength you need to push through the nausea, the aches and pains, the heartburn, the smell sensitivity . . . all of it. Whatever you're facing today, God is with you, and He can help you endure and continue onward, one day at a time.

Lord God,
thank You for another day. Each day is a gift,
no matter how I feel. I pray for strength to
get through today. Tomorrow is in Your hands.
Thank You for promising to be with me
each and every moment.
Amen.

Miracle in the Making | 43

Smiling Through the Pain

So stop telling lies. Let us tell our neighbors the truth, for we are all parts of the same body.
EPHESIANS 4:25 NLT

We kept my pregnancy a secret for weeks and weeks during my first trimester. Going to church, serving on Wednesday nights with the youth group, and attending meetings and trainings at work were draining in a way I had never experienced. I often had to excuse myself and run to the bathroom to breathe through nausea if someone walked by with a strong perfume or a take-out dinner. People asked me why I wasn't eating at meals or why I continued to cancel plans. On the outside, I tried to look put together and composed. I smiled through meetings at my new job. I hid the nausea wristbands with long-sleeved shirts. I pretended that everything was fine. But inside, I was a wreck. Not only did I feel terrible most of the time, but I was also drowning in bouts of depression, anxiety, and uncertainty about my future.

There are good reasons for keeping your pregnancy quiet in the early days. But don't do what I did. Be open with someone about how you're really feeling. Ask for help when you're too exhausted to volunteer. Be honest. Sometimes our attempt to smile through the pain is just hurting us more. God is right by your side, always. Be honest with Him, but also find people who can help you through this season in your life. Throughout your pregnancy, it's okay to tell the truth about what you're feeling. Yes, pregnancy is a wonderful gift. But it's also very hard, stressful, and exhausting at times. There is no shame in admitting that to someone who genuinely asks how you're doing. You don't have to pretend.

God,
I want to tell You how I'm truly feeling.
I know You want to hear my thoughts and fears,
and I know You understand.
Bring someone into my life who will listen
and encourage me during the months ahead.
Amen.

Learning from Jesus' Sacrifice

Though He was God, He did not think of equality with God as something to cling to. Instead, He gave up His divine privileges; He took the humble position of a slave and was born as a human being. When He appeared in human form, He humbled Himself in obedience to God and died a criminal's death on a cross.
PHILIPPIANS 2:6–8 NLT

What exactly is *sacrifice*? According to Merriam-Webster's dictionary, *sacrifice* means the "destruction or surrender of something for the sake of something else" or "something given up or lost." Both definitions adequately describe what Jesus did for us. Philippians 2:7 says that Jesus "gave up His divine privileges" and "was born as a human being." He sacrificed His divine rights to become a humble human servant and live among us. He chose to walk in obedience. Ultimately, Jesus sacrificed His own life and died a criminal's death on a cross so we could experience eternal freedom from sin. What Jesus endured is hard to fully grasp, but He willingly surrendered His own life for our sake. Why? Because He loved us that much.

Though we can never completely comprehend the weight of His sacrifice for us, becoming a parent might be the closest we can get to understanding what sacrificial love truly is. Jesus surrendered His divine privileges to come to earth as a human man. He gave up His very life and endured excruciating pain and suffering on the cross before He rose again. What you are currently enduring during pregnancy is the beginning of a lifelong sacrifice for your child. You are giving up your body for the sake of your baby. You are surrendering your freedom, your time, and even your dignity (at times) for the healthy growth and delivery of that new, tiny life. You're following in Christ's footsteps by sacrificing now so your child can live. As you walk through suffering during pregnancy, allow it to remind you of what Jesus willingly endured for your sake. While you won't have to experience death on the cross, you are dying to yourself, to your own ambitions, for the baby growing inside of you. Motherhood *is* sacrifice, and it starts right now.

Jesus,

my heart is full of gratitude for what You chose to endure for my sake. Thank You for sacrificing so that I could live. I want to follow Your example and live out sacrificial love for my baby. Help me to stay strong.

Amen.

Laboring for Your Child

It will be like a woman suffering the pains of labor. When her child is born, her anguish gives way to joy because she has brought a new baby into the world.
JOHN 16:21 NLT

In John 16, Jesus is speaking to His disciples about His impending arrest, crucifixion, and resurrection. He tells them that they will experience grief and sadness because of what will happen to Him, but then they will experience joy after He comes back from the dead. To illustrate this picture, He uses the example of a woman in childbirth. There is initial suffering as the woman undergoes labor pains, but then she is filled with joy because "she has brought a new baby into the world." Even thousands of years ago, the disciples could understand this picture well and immediately understood what Jesus was trying to say.

Labor and delivery have changed with modern medicine, and that is something we can be thankful for! But, however you choose to give birth, you will undoubtedly experience some pain during the process of bringing your child into this world. Instead of fretting about the pain that might come, focus instead on the joy that is promised afterward. You'll be overcome with happiness when they put your new baby in your arms. Everything—all the pain from labor, all the months of discomfort, all the preparation and sleepless nights—will be so worth it.

You are shouldering a bit of suffering for the sake of your child. Children may never fully understand this sacrifice until they are old enough to be parents themselves. But it will always be the first great act of love that you will show your baby. So don't allow fear and anxiety to take over when you think about labor. Instead, focus on the immense joy that comes immediately after the suffering. With God by your side, you are so much stronger than you think.

Dear God,

I leave my worries about labor with You. While I might experience pain, it will all be worth it when I get to hold my baby. Help me to have courage as I look toward my due date.

Amen.

What Is True Love?

See what kind of love the Father has given to us, that we should be called children of God; and so we are. The reason why the world does not know us is that it did not know him.

I JOHN 3:1 ESV

From pop music to romance novels to animated movies, people have tried to describe "true love" at its purest level. But in most cases, they don't get it right. Why? Because true love was designed and defined by God Himself. First John 3:1 implores us to "see what kind of love the Father has given to us." Our model for true love comes straight from the Father and the sacrifice of His Son. The Greek word for "love" in this particular verse is *agapé*. It's not a word to describe romantic love or your affection for chocolate. It's an all-encompassing, divine sort of love that's given while expecting nothing in return. What a truly amazing thing that God has this kind of love for us, His children.

When we follow in the footsteps of Jesus, we are asked to exhibit this same *agapé* love for our family, our friends, our neighbors, and even complete strangers. It's a type of love that requires service, patience, and perseverance, and it can sometimes hurt deeply when it's never given back. Pregnancy is a time when you are giving *agapé* love each and every day, even if you don't realize it. You are loving your baby by sacrificing your energy, emotions, and body. During pregnancy and for years after, your child won't be able to give you the same love back. But you will pour out all the love you have in your body just the same. That's what is so incredible about motherhood. It teaches us something fundamental about the God who created us. He is also pouring out His *agapé* love for you and for your child, even if you don't ever think to give it back to Him. Pregnancy gives us just a little taste of what the purest love on earth can be.

Father,
thank You for loving me with Your agapé love.
I don't deserve it, but You give it anyway.
Help me to pour out the same true love for my baby
in the months and years ahead. I love You, Lord.
Amen.

The Dichotomy of Pregnancy Emotion

> For everything there is a season, and a time for every matter under heaven . . . a time to weep, and a time to laugh; a time to mourn, and a time to dance.
> **ECCLESIASTES 3:1, 4 ESV**

Think about your average day. You might wake up feeling hopeful for the day ahead. You go through the first few hours and feel cheerful. Then, perhaps you experience some nausea or a burst of pain in your back or hips. Your mood sours. You get frustrated with your husband or your coworkers. Your feet hurt, but you still have to stand up to give a presentation or prepare lunch for your family. You're tired, but you can't quit your job or take a nap in a conference room. Then, in mid-afternoon, you read something sweet on social media or watch a heartwarming video, and suddenly you're weeping quietly in the bathroom with no way to control the flow of tears. You finally end the day worn out physically and emotionally, go home, and face bills, think about your birth plan, walk into the empty nursery that still isn't set up yet, and . . .

Welcome to the whirlwind of pregnancy emotions.

Sometimes we feel like we experience the entirety of Ecclesiastes 3:4 in the span of a few hours. It says that there is "a time to weep, and a time to laugh; a time to mourn, and a time to dance." There are high mountaintops and low valleys in our emotions, and it's okay. God created our hormones for a particular reason, and they can do some pretty crazy things during pregnancy. It's okay to feel bursts of warm excitement when you look down at your swelling belly. And it's also okay to feel cold panic at the thought of actually having a child. Communicate with your husband, your family, and your support group. Tell them, "Today, I'm feeling . . . " When you have bursts of random anger, take a few moments by yourself to gather your thoughts and pray before you speak harshly. When you have bouts of crying that make no sense, let the tears flow and tell yourself that it's just temporary. Your crazy emotions are just one part of this journey that you're on, and it won't last forever.

Dear Lord,

sometimes I feel like I'm on a roller coaster of emotion.
Help me to watch my words when I'm angry.
Thank You for the moments of cheerful joy.
Walk with me through all the ups and downs
that I'm feeling.

Amen.

Savoring Moments

> Enter His gates with thanksgiving and His courts
> with praise. Give thanks to Him and bless His name.
> For the LORD is good, and His faithful love endures
> forever; His faithfulness, through all generations.
> PSALM 100:4–5 CSB

Are you solely focused on the future, or are you embracing the present? It's easy to think about pregnancy as a hurdle that you have to get over in order to get to the future you really want. Of course, there is a finish line, and that is holding your baby in your arms. Days of pregnancy are filled with aches, nausea, stress, and emotions. Who would want to stay in this season long-term? But you must remember that each and every day is a gift that you cannot get back.

First, learn now to savor moments, even the hard ones. Someday you'll look back on these days with a hint of fondness. One day, this baby you're carrying inside of you will be walking across the stage at graduation, walking down the aisle at their wedding, and holding their own baby in their arms as you look on. And you'll think back to these days and wonder how time passed so quickly.

Second, live each day in the present. This can be difficult when you are so eager for time to pass. But you aren't in the future yet. You're here, right now, and God has something to show you and teach you today.

Third, you can give thanks. King David writes in Psalm 100:4, "Give thanks to Him and bless His name." When you wake up (even on mornings when you feel sick), say a short prayer of thanks for another day, and ask God to show you what He wants to teach you. When you have big milestones like an ultrasound or a baby shower, soak it all in and hide those memories in your heart for the future. Remember to thank the Lord for what He has given you.

You are a mother! You have a little, precious life growing inside of you. Today is a wonderful gift. Despite the difficulties that lie ahead, you can still savor the moment, live in the present, and give thanks for what you have.

Jesus,
thank You for another day. Thank You for this baby You've blessed me with. Thank You for the memories I'll make during pregnancy that I'll remember for the rest of my life. You are so faithful.
Amen.

Miracle in the Making | 55

The Strongest Defense

*Put on all of God's armor so that you will be able
to stand firm against all strategies of the devil.
For we are not fighting against flesh-and-blood enemies,
but against evil rulers and authorities of the unseen
world, against mighty powers in this dark world,
and against evil spirits in the heavenly places.*
EPHESIANS 6:11–12 NLT

Have you ever heard this saying used in sports or in the military: "The best defense is a good offense"? It's a strategic way of defending your own territory, goal, or team. When you play good offense, the opposing side will be so occupied with keeping up and defending their own turf that they won't be able to target your team.

In many ways, we are in a strategic military battle with "evil rulers and authorities of the unseen world" each and every day. The theater of war? Our minds. We can get so comfortable in our daily lives that we forget there are forces who seek to do us harm. In John 10:10 (NLT), Jesus says that a "thief" wants "to steal and kill and destroy." The easiest way for him to battle against us is to twist our thoughts away from God; to plant seeds of doubt, anger, and bitterness; and to keep us focused only on ourselves.

During pregnancy, we are especially vulnerable. Our minds are full of fearful thoughts, and our emotions are ripe for manipulation. We can be so easily distracted by our physical symptoms and our own individual lives that we never think about God.

Ephesians 6:11–12 tells you how to have a good offense. You are to "put on all of God's armor so that you will be able to stand firm." Read Ephesians 6:10–17 and take note of every piece of armor that is needed for this fight. When angry thoughts come into your mind, when you start to doubt, or when you realize that you've been distracted and far from God, fight back through prayer and reading Scripture.

God,

remind me of the battle for my heart and mind.
Help me to put on Your armor to fight against the enemy.
I'm grateful I'm on the winning side of this war.

Amen.

The Great Wait

The LORD is good to those who wait for Him,
to the person who seeks Him.
It is good to wait quietly for salvation from the LORD.
LAMENTATIONS 3:25–26 CSB

Ready . . . set . . . wait!

Waiting is never easy. We see it easily in children when they are told to wait their turn in line. It's our human nature to be impatient. But there is nothing that tests your patience quite like pregnancy. From the moment you read your pregnancy test result to the moment you see your baby for the first time, there are months and months of waiting.

My husband's greatest wish in life is to be a father. For years and years, even before we met, he'd been looking forward to getting to be a dad. I wasn't as sure about the idea of parenthood, but we decided after a few years of marriage that we wanted to try to have a child. He was ecstatic when we received the news that I was pregnant. Immediately, he was on a mission of research and planning, even though it was so early.

Throughout the long months of pregnancy, we both struggled with impatience, him even more so than me. The dream he'd wanted for so long was finally within reach, but it still hadn't come to fruition. By the time I was in my third trimester, we swore that time had started going backward. Every day felt like it was stretching longer and longer. My due date was worlds away and unreachable. When I reached thirty-six weeks, my husband's "go bag" was already packed, zipped, and sitting by the door. He was ready. Ready to wait some more, as it turned out.

In Galatians 5:22, "patience" is listed as a fruit of the Spirit. It's something that you can obtain by leaning into God and His Word. It's not easy, but growing in patience helps you become more and more like Jesus. God wants to teach you patience during this pregnancy. As long as the months may seem, they truly will end. God's timing for your child is better than your timing. So while you are waiting, thank the Lord for the opportunity to learn patience.

Jesus,

thank You for teaching me how to be patient while I'm waiting for my child to be born. Help me through the long days when time feels like it's going so slowly. Every day is a gift from You. I can wait a little longer.

Amen.

Centering Your Thoughts

Finally brothers and sisters, whatever is true, whatever is honorable, whatever is just, whatever is pure, whatever is lovely, whatever is commendable—if there is any moral excellence and if there is anything praiseworthy— dwell on these things.

PHILIPPIANS 4:8 CSB

Our minds are a battleground. If we're not careful, our thoughts can become filled with anxiety, fears, doubt, and frustration. And before we know it, our minds become so focused on all the bad things that could happen that we forget to focus on God. It's a constant struggle to keep our minds on God, but that's what God asks of us and it's what is ultimately best for our mental health. Colossians 3:2 (CSB) says, "Set your minds on things above, not on earthly things." Romans 12:2 (CSB) says, "Do not be conformed to this age, but be transformed by the renewing of your mind, so that you may discern what is the good, pleasing, and perfect will of God." Over and over again in Scripture, we can see the importance of protecting and strengthening our thoughts. How can we fight against the temptation to dwell on anxiety, fears, lust, or doubt? How about asking

God to redirect them to something else? Philippians 4:8 lists out what we should recenter our minds on. Think about things that are true, honorable, just, pure, lovely, commendable, morally excellent, and praiseworthy.

It's easy during pregnancy to allow our mental fortitude to slip up. Hateful thoughts can sneak in. Surging hormones can turn desire into lust. Normal worries and fears can become a raging monster of anxiety that keeps your mind entrapped instead of set free. Don't give up the battle for your mind. Start your days with prayer and reading Scripture. Then, when the attacks begin in the middle of the night, remind yourself of those verses you read and center your thoughts on God. Push aside those worst-case scenarios and focus instead on pure and lovely thoughts about God, your life, and your baby.

Dear God,
please help me keep my mind steadfast and centered on You. Help me not to buckle under the stress and pressure of my thoughts, but to know that You are caring for me. Help me to keep my mind set on good, pure things.
Amen.

Holding on to Contentment

I don't say this out of need, for I have learned to be content in whatever circumstances I find myself.
PHILIPPIANS 4:11 CSB

True contentment is what every person really wants in life. People spend so much money in the search for contentment. Some invest in cars or sports. Others obsess over current fashion, going on the best vacations, or buying the nicest house—the list goes on. Many of us fall prey to the "appearance" of contentment that we see on social media.

It doesn't end when we become pregnant. We see friends or acquaintances having babies and making it look like a walk in the park. We read blog posts of other moms gushing over their love of pregnancy, and we feel like something is wrong with us. We scroll through endless social media pictures of people living their "best lives" with all the bells and whistles of the "shiny" and "new" and "fashion-forward." But most likely, those people aren't showing the reality that they are living, and they probably aren't *really* as content as they seem. So how do we discover this elusive contentment in life?

The first step is to realize that contentment isn't about obtaining more. It's realizing that we already have everything we need. The apostle Paul had a tough life of poverty, persecution, and struggle. But in Philippians 4:11, he writes that "I have learned to be content in whatever circumstances I find myself." He found true contentment through his relationship with Jesus Christ and not through anything the world offered him.

Joni Eareckson Tada, the founder of the Joni & Friends ministry, became a quadriplegic at the age of seventeen after a diving accident. She is unable to move any part of her body below her neck. And yet, she has touched the lives of thousands of people through her ministry. She says, "For me, true contentment on earth means asking less of this life because more is coming in the next." When we have Jesus, we have everything we need. It's tough to feel content during the trials of pregnancy, but whatever we face, we can follow Paul's example and learn how to be content.

Jesus,

I do believe that You are all I need. Thank You for providing me with so many good gifts in my life. Help me to look at what I already have instead of chasing after false happiness. Help me to rest in contentment today.

Amen.

Balancing Busyness

> The LORD answered her, "Martha, Martha, you are worried and upset about many things, but one thing is necessary. Mary has made the right choice, and it will not be taken away from her."
>
> LUKE 10:41–42 CSB

If you read the full story of Martha and Mary in Luke 10:38–42, you'll find that Martha was busy. She was stressed. She felt overwhelmed and overlooked. Does that sound familiar? It's important to note that nothing Martha did was wrong. In fact, in the first century, it would have been a huge honor for her to welcome a great teacher like Jesus of Nazareth into her home. She wanted to be a good hostess and serve her guests well.

Sometimes your schedule is full of good things and activities that need to happen. You might be focused on your job and working right up until the baby comes. You might be involved in many volunteer or service projects that take up time outside of the workday. You probably feel the need to clean the house, prepare meals, and check things off your baby to-do list. None of these things is bad in nature. But busyness can start with good intentions and end up cutting off your direct connection to the Savior. That's what happened to Martha.

Martha was frustrated that her sister, Mary, was not concerned about being a good hostess. Martha might have been a little too preoccupied with the "perfect image" instead of learning from the teacher Himself. She became so angry that she walked into His teaching moment and interrupted Him, demanding that He force Mary to help her in the kitchen. When life gets so busy that we can't keep our heads above water, we can tend to demand things of God without listening in return. Martha forgot who was in her home. Her toils and tasks could wait. Jesus tells her in verse 42 that "one thing is necessary." Spending time at His feet was the most important thing, and everything else could fall by the wayside. Busyness is inevitable in this life, but it doesn't have to be all-consuming. While you're juggling your tasks and your to-dos, don't forget to make time to simply sit at Jesus' feet.

Dear Jesus,

I can become so easily distracted by menial tasks in this life. I can be a Martha, when I really need to put aside time to be a Mary. Thank You for the reminder that You are always there, ready to teach me if I am ready to listen.

Amen.

Straight from the Garden

> Then He said to the woman, "I will sharpen the pain
> of your pregnancy, and in pain you will give birth.
> And you will desire to control your husband,
> but he will rule over you."
> **GENESIS 3:16 NLT**

We've always learned that Eve was cursed with pain in labor due to her personal sin in the Garden of Eden. But have you ever thought that maybe Eve's primary sin was *control*? She fell into the temptation of controlling her own destiny and gaining the knowledge that God had forbidden. In many ways, painful pregnancies and childbirth were a just punishment for her actions because there is so little that we can control about our pregnancy and labor.

The second part of verse 16 states that Eve would "desire to control [her] husband." The desire to control stretches much further than marriage. We want to know and understand exactly what will happen and when in many areas of our life. So before you go straight to blaming Eve for the pain and discomfort you feel right now, take a moment to focus inward. Are you that different from Eve? Wouldn't you snatch up the opportunity to look into a crystal ball and know exactly what will happen for your pregnancy and for your baby?

God uses pregnancy and childbirth to remind us that we are never in control. He is. It's so hard to change our perspective, in the area of control, but giving it up is what is ultimately best for us. It's pushing against our very sin nature of holding tightly and refusing to let go. Let your aches, pains, and discomforts gently remind you to turn control back to God and to walk in trust today.

God,

I want to believe that I'm in control, but I'm not. I can't control my pregnancy or the birth of my child. But You promise that You will never leave me nor forsake me. Please draw near to me today and help me fight against the sin nature of control.

Amen.

Raising a Child in Today's World

> "I have said these things to you, that in me
> you may have peace. In the world you will have
> tribulation. But take heart; I have overcome the world."
> JOHN 16:33 ESV

Just like there is very little we can do to control pregnancy or childbirth, there is very little we can do to control what our children will experience in this world. They will see evil done and sins committed. They will face trials and suffering. As a mother, that's a terrifying thought. No one wants to face suffering, and we want to protect our innocent babies so much more than we want to protect ourselves. Even during a first pregnancy, these thoughts might have surfaced. How can we expect to raise our children up to know and love God in such an imperfect, sometimes-scary world? What will life look like for our kids when they get to be adults? What can we expect in the years to come? How can we prepare our children in the best way we can?

John 16:33 (ESV) gives us strength and hope when Jesus says, "in me you may have peace. In the world you will have tribulation. But take heart; I have overcome the world." Despite all the bad things that occur in the news and across the globe, we know the true Victor in the story—

Jesus. He is stronger than the brokenness. His disciples faced endless persecution and suffering after Jesus returned to heaven, but they didn't give up. As scary as it is to raise our children in today's world, we know that we are equipping them with the true light: the light of Christ.

Jesus,

I need Your peace as I look at the world around me.
Help me teach my child how to navigate this place.
Give me wisdom on how to raise my children. We need You.

Amen.

The True Creator of Life

You made all the delicate, inner parts of my body and knit me together in my mother's womb.
PSALM 139:13 NLT

Mothers have an amazing role in the bringing of new life into our world. A baby's life begins so small that we can't see it with the naked eye. And somehow, over the course of nine months, that tiny little life grows and grows into a living, breathing (screaming) baby. In many ways, we are artists working on a masterpiece.

When you see your baby for the first time, he or she will look absolutely perfect to you. A work of art. A miracle. And those hands and feet and beautiful eyes and lips formed and grew *inside of you*. Many cultures around the world revere women for being the creators of life. Many polytheistic religions have "goddesses of fertility" to which they pray when they have trouble conceiving. But women don't create life. You and the baby's father didn't actually create life together, even though it might seem like it.

God is the true Creator of life. He's the true Master Artist working on the masterpiece inside of us. We get to be vessels for His artwork, and what an honor that is.

Women should be honored and respected for our part in bringing new life into the world. It's hard work. But we must always acknowledge who the real Creator is.

God is slowly, piece by piece, knitting your child together right now. He created your body to be a safe place for this miracle to occur. You were made to do this. Out of all the billions of people who have lived on earth in the last few thousand years, none will ever be exactly like your baby. Your baby will be a unique creation, and only God can do that. Next time you feel a bit nauseous or fatigued, remind yourself that your body is working alongside our Maker to create something beautiful and new. What an amazing privilege that we get to be tools in the Master Artist's hands.

God,

thank You for carefully knitting my child together during this time of pregnancy. You are the true Creator of life, not me. Thank You for taking such special care with every detail in my baby's body. I trust that You are in control.

Amen.

Cutting Down on Complaining

Do everything without complaining and arguing, so that no one can criticize you. Live clean, innocent lives as children of God, shining like bright lights in a world full of crooked and perverse people.
PHILIPPIANS 2:14–15 NLT

We have all caught ourselves complaining about the smallest things. The wear and tear that pregnancy takes on our bodies, along with the fatigue, can also cause us to become short-tempered, impatient, and impractical at times. While we don't have to pretend that we are fine when we don't feel well, we also must be careful not to fall into the temptation of complaining.

At first, we think we are being honest with someone about how we feel. Then, it starts to spread like an infection. We start complaining about how much we don't enjoy pregnancy. We're complaining that our husbands are not being supportive enough. We're complaining about how our symptoms seem way worse than anyone else's. Complaining tends to fester until it's our knee-jerk reaction to any question. It's okay to be honest about how we feel. But it's another thing to have negativity running so deep that a complaint is always on the surface, whether it's about an aching back or the wait time at a restaurant.

Paul writes in Philippians 2:14–15 that we should "do everything without complaining" and to "live clean, innocent lives as children of God." The problem with complaining is not so much about how we come across to others, but what it does to our own hearts. When we succumb to this habit, it creates ingratitude. We become so "me"-focused that we forget to be grateful for all the good things that are happening. We can allow negativity to become a storm cloud that hangs over our heads and steals the joys that come with pregnancy. No one is perfect, and we will all have complaints about our aches, pains, and discomforts. But don't stay there. Remind yourself of the good things you *do* have. Remind yourself of the symptoms that you *don't* have. Say a prayer of gratitude when the temptation to complain comes your way.

Lord,
it's so easy to complain when I don't feel at my best.
But there is so much I have to be grateful for.
Help me set my mind on the good things I have instead
of focusing on the negative during this season.
Amen.

Embracing Seasons

> Lord, remind me how brief my time on earth will be.
> Remind me that my days are numbered—how fleeting
> my life is. You have made my life no longer than the
> width of my hand. My entire lifetime is just a moment
> to you; at best, each of us is but a breath.
> PSALM 39:4–5 NLT

Take a moment to walk down memory lane. Close your eyes and think about some key seasons in your life. Spend some time thinking about your childhood and your adolescent years. What did you learn? What were some trials that you faced? How did you grow? Then, think about graduating from high school and moving into those young adult years. Remember what it was like to get your first paycheck? Or the stress of paying all your bills on your own? Focus on some happy memories that you want to hold close to your heart today. Remember good times with your parents or siblings. Time can make it easy to forget the bad memories. Our minds automatically want to bring up the good things that happened in our past. Our childhoods weren't perfect, but we can still pick out the sweet memories.

Life is really a series of seasons. Time moves so fast, doesn't it? We blink, and another year has passed. We hit another birthday and think, *How is it possible that I'm now this old?* Psalm 39:4–5 reminds us how short our lives are in the span of eternity. Verse 5 says "each of us is but a breath."

Think of each and every season that passes as a gift. Every season has something unique and special to teach you about God, about yourself, and about life. Grab a journal during these weeks of pregnancy and write down what this specific season is teaching you. As hard as it is right now, someday you'll look back and remember mostly the good things about pregnancy. You'll remember those first little kicks. That first sonogram. The feeling of love when you looked down at your swelling tummy. Seasons come and go, and we may not experience them again. So savor this pregnancy for the true gift from God that it is.

Dear God,

thank You for giving me this gift of pregnancy. Help me to learn from it and grow during these months and weeks. Grant me the endurance I need to push through. I want to hold the good things tight to my heart.

Amen.

A Daily Dose of Gratitude

> Rejoice always, pray constantly, give thanks in
> everything; for this is God's will for you in Christ Jesus.
> I THESSALONIANS 5:16–18 csb

What were your first thoughts when you woke up and rolled out of bed this morning? Depending on how far along you are in your pregnancy, your thoughts could have been: *Another morning of nausea* . . . or *How am I already so hungry?* or *Ouch, there are those achy hips and back.* Mornings tend to be hard for pregnant women. The larger your belly grows, the harder it is to push yourself out of bed. Some women experience acute morning sickness for their entire pregnancies. Where the smell of brewed coffee used to bring a simple joy in the morning, it could now cause a surge of nausea or bring about heartburn.

Instead of morning coffee, what if you decided to have a daily dose of gratitude? It only takes a few seconds, but it can reset the tone for your entire day. Once you get up and around, close your eyes and say a quick prayer of thanks for something unique and special that day. Maybe it's thanking God for a day of cooler weather. Or it could be giving thanks for a good night's sleep if that has been difficult. There is *always* something to give thanks about, even if it's simply being grateful for another day of life.

A daily dose of gratitude can shift your perspective to be one of positivity and joy. While you may be experiencing some intense pregnancy symptoms, there are always symptoms that you *don't* have. Be thankful for that! Set your mind first thing in the morning to gratitude, and you'll find that the aches and pains don't bother you as much. Rejoice in another new day that you get to carry your child and help him or her grow into a healthy baby. Each and every day is a beautiful gift from God.

Lord,
thank You for a new morning and a new sunrise. Thank You for the privilege of carrying this new life inside of me. Thank You for another day of life and experiences.
Amen.

Leaning on Your Husband

> In the same way, you husbands must give honor to your wives. Treat your wife with understanding as you live together. She may be weaker than you are, but she is your equal partner in God's gift of new life. Treat her as you should so your prayers will not be hindered.
> 1 PETER 3:7 NLT

No marriage is perfect, and no husband is perfect either. The stresses of a new pregnancy can pull out the negatives and strains in your marriage in ways that very little else can. Your husband is also experiencing a multitude of emotions, just like you. He might be panicked about the idea of another baby to provide for. Or he might be overjoyed with excitement but struggling with insecurity about being a dad. Give grace to one another during these months but take the opportunity to draw together for mutual support. If this is your first pregnancy, you're closing a chapter on time spent with just each other. You're going from a family of two to a family of three, and things will look different from now on. Embrace these last few months of just being two. Try to go on dates or walks. Soak up evenings when it's just the two of you on the couch watching a movie. This is a sweet time of preparation for you both, and it's a beautiful thing to become first-time parents together.

If this is not your first pregnancy, rely on your husband to assist with the other kids while you walk through the difficulties of pregnancy. Lean on each other for strength. Be open and honest on the hard days and rejoice together on the good days. If you do not have a husband during this season of your life, find a tight-knit support group that can walk with you each and every day. God made us social creatures. We don't have to do this life alone.

Dear Lord,

thank You for giving me my husband [or my support group]. Please help me know how to lean on him in times of weakness and to encourage him when he needs to be lifted up. Strengthen our marriage during the months ahead so we are strong and ready for a new baby.

Amen.

Let the Tears Fall

You yourself have recorded my wanderings.
Put my tears in Your bottle. Are they not in Your book?
Then my enemies will retreat on the day when I call.
This I know: God is for me.
PSALM 56:8–9 CSB

Pregnancy is a time when it's important to learn how to give grace to yourself. There is so much going on in your body, and it's hard to tell which way is up some days. Your emotions are hard to wrangle. Your body hurts. It might be difficult to eat your favorite foods or enjoy holiday meals with the family. Sometimes you might need to go into your bedroom and cry to release some of the plugged-up emotions of the day. And you know what? God sees each and every tear. Many of the psalms that David wrote are filled with recordings of him weeping and crying out to God in distress or grief. There is no weakness in letting tears fall. Jesus Himself wept for His friends. It's okay to cry.

On those really hard days when you feel completely run dry and worn out, remember Psalm 56:9; "This I know: God is for me." Let yourself feel frustration, pain, and sadness during these months. You might cry more in pregnancy than you've ever cried before in your life. And God is for you and with you. Allow Him to comfort you when you feel too weak to continue on. Allow Him to bring others in to encourage and uplift you when you feel down. Sometimes your hormones will bring about tears that you don't even understand and can't explain, and that's okay too! So let yourself cry in that movie even though no one else is. Shed a few tears when you look at those adorable baby clothes. Cry it out when you're tired and sore and weary of pregnancy. Then remember that God is with you and for you. You can get back up and keep going with His strength.

Lord,

thank You that You number each of my tears and understand exactly how I feel, even when no one else does. Give me the strength to continue, even as I allow myself to experience the full breadth of emotions that come with pregnancy.

Amen.

Learning to Forgive

Put on then, as God's chosen ones, holy and beloved, compassionate hearts, kindness, humility, meekness, and patience, bearing with one another and, if one has a complaint against another, forgiving each other; as the Lord has forgiven you, so you also must forgive.
COLOSSIANS 3:12–13 ESV

I was twenty-eight years old when I looked down at that positive pregnancy test. My first thought was: *I'm too young to be a parent. I'm practically a kid myself.* No one feels particularly ready to be a mom or dad at first. Even though I'm firmly in my adult years, it's still hard to think of myself as a responsible grown-up at times. Walking through pregnancy made me look at my own parents a bit differently. Most of us carry some hurt from our childhoods. No parent is perfect. Even if we had wonderful moms or dads and fantastic memories, we could still be holding on to some hurts. In reality, our parents probably felt the same way—they felt like kids themselves when they had us. They didn't have it all together, just like you don't now. None of us is perfect, and you're also going to make mistakes in parenting.

It's time to forgive. Forgiveness is never an easy thing. But for the most part, your parents were probably doing their best and simply messed up at times. Whether you grew up in a two-parent household or you experienced a divorce during your childhood, let this be a time when you put the past to rest and give grace to your parents. Your story will not be their story. You'll make your own mistakes, and you'll need to rely on God to lead you through the trials of parenting. Maybe it's time to release the pain and bitterness toward your own parents and experience freedom.

Lord,
help me to forgive my parents. Just like me,
they were just young people having a kid and trying to
figure it out. Help me to give them grace and forgiveness.
I need You each day to be the best parent I can be.
Amen.

Comparison and Bitterness

For you are still controlled by your sinful nature. You are jealous of one another and quarrel with each other. Doesn't that prove you are controlled by your sinful nature? Aren't you living like people of the world?
I CORINTHIANS 3:3 NLT

President Theodore Roosevelt said, "Comparison is the thief of joy." You've probably heard that quote before, but let the truth of that statement sink in. The Tenth Commandment is "do not covet" (Exodus 20:17). When we compare ourselves, our bodies, and our circumstances to others, we are automatically coveting what they have and forgetting the blessings that we do have. The more we look to others in comparison, the less we live in joy and confidence in our own lives.

Pregnancy is a hard time to avoid comparison. Every woman's body is affected differently. Some women don't gain much weight during the gestational months, while others do. Some women don't have many symptoms at all, while others experience the full gamut. Some women have relatively easy births, while others may have a difficult time in labor or perhaps need a C-section. No one will have the exact same experience during pregnancy and labor.

Paul rebukes the Corinthian church in I Corinthians 3:3, saying, "You are jealous of one another. . . . Aren't you living like people of the world?" As we follow Christ's example, we must let go of comparison, jealousy, and coveting. You may not look or feel exactly like yourself right now, and that is okay. Your experience is completely your own. So don't fall into the temptation to compare your body or your circumstances with other women around you. Instead, be thankful for the body that God gave you and the experiences that you get to cherish and remember during pregnancy. Comparison can so easily lead to bitterness toward God, yourself, and those closest to you. Even when you're having a difficult time and it feels like you're the only one experiencing difficulty, remember that you're not alone. Many women have gone before you, and God is always with you. No one else will have *your* story.

Lord Jesus,
please help me avoid comparison with others during my pregnancy. I feel vulnerable right now, and I need Your help to stay confident. You gave me this child and this pregnancy for a reason. I trust You.
Amen.

Embracing Your New Body

> No one hates his own body but feeds and cares for it,
> just as Christ cares for the church.
> **EPHESIANS 5:29 NLT**

Your body is going through a series of major changes during these months. It's truly a miracle how God created a woman's body to care for and nurture a growing baby. But there are hard changes as well, and almost all of these adjustments are out of our control. Some things will go away after birth, but other changes may stick around for the rest of your life. As the months progress and your tummy grows, you may see stretch marks appear. Some women get spiderlike veins that materialize and don't go away. Your hair may change texture. Your skin might have some unique coloration for a time. Your fingers and feet might swell and look a little different. After birth, you might have a C-section scar, and every woman experiences excess skin on the belly after delivery. Right now, it might be hard to look in the mirror and love what you see.

But you should.

You are doing something incredible that only a mother can do. You're sacrificing your comfort, your energy, and your past appearance to bring something so special into this world. You are a warrior, and every warrior has a few battle scars. Be proud of those marks on your belly or the web of veins on your thighs. They are marks of strength and perseverance. Your body may never be exactly the same as it was pre-pregnancy, but you can learn to love your new body and embrace the changes that come. Go out and find some fun maternity outfits that you like. Fix your hair to explore the new textures. Buy some comfy shoes that allow more room for swollen feet. When you look in the mirror and feel discouraged by the changes you see, remember that you are incredibly strong and beautiful. God made your body to do this, and all the battle scars you wear when it's over will be worth the life of your baby. You are always a masterpiece, and you can learn to love and respect the new body you'll have at the end.

God,

thank You for creating my body to be strong throughout pregnancy. Sometimes it's hard to love myself with all these changes, but I know Your love for me is unconditional. Teach me how to love myself unconditionally too.

Amen.

Treating Yourself with Kindness

*A friend loves at all times,
and a brother is born for a difficult time.*
PROVERBS 17:17 csb

Take a moment to ponder what phrases or thoughts you've been telling yourself during these past few weeks or months of pregnancy. Have you been critical of yourself and your body? Have you looked in the mirror and thought something degrading about how you look? We can say the most horrible things to ourselves in our own private thoughts. *I'm getting so fat. These stretch marks are so ugly. I'll never look beautiful again after this. I can't stand to look at myself in the mirror.*

Now, imagine that you go to your best friend's house, sit down with her, and tell her these exact same things straight to her face—about *her*. Can you imagine yourself ever telling someone else the things you say to yourself? Of course not! We would never treat our friends the way we treat and critique ourselves. We are our own worst critics, and we can fill our minds with so many unkind and degrading thoughts about our bodies, our personalities, and our circumstances that we walk around without confidence, feeling defeated. We grab a stick to beat over our own heads instead of stepping back and putting everything into perspective.

What if we treated ourselves like we would treat a dear friend?

Proverbs 17:17 says, "A friend loves at all times." If a pregnant friend came to you, sat down in tears, and said, "I feel like I can't even look in the mirror anymore. I just hate what I see," what would you say in return? Would you encourage her? Give her a warm hug? Tell her that she's so incredibly beautiful no matter how her appearance may change these next few months?

Why can't we treat ourselves with the same kindness? Next time a harsh thought sweeps in or you feel a burst of low self-esteem, tell yourself all the things you would tell your friend. Quote encouraging Scriptures. Say a prayer of gratitude for this body that you have. Remind yourself that what you see is temporary, and the result of your struggle—your baby—will be so worth it.

Lord,

help me to treat myself with kindness.
You built me for this, and Your opinions of me
never change. Help me to treat myself like
I would treat a friend and give myself some grace.

Amen.

A Routine of Rest

Then Jesus said, "Come to Me, all of you who are weary and carry heavy burdens, and I will give you rest. Take My yoke upon you. Let Me teach you, because I am humble and gentle at heart, and you will find rest for your souls. For My yoke is easy to bear, and the burden I give you is light."
MATTHEW 11:28–30 NLT

Did you know that God commanded the Israelites to rest? In Exodus 20:10, God ordered the Israelites to keep the Sabbath as a day of rest and honor Him without work being done. Today, many of us work five days a week and have a weekend that we get to stay home. But it's very rare that our weekends or our Sunday "Sabbath" is actually restful. As you grow in your pregnancy, you'll feel incredibly weary. When you embark on your third trimester, the "heavy burden" will become very real as you carry the extra weight of a growing baby in your tummy.

God wants us to establish a routine of rest, and not just for our bodies. He wants us to set aside protected time each week to take a break from busyness, to refresh ourselves, and to focus on Him. Find a time in your schedule when you can simply rest at home without any work or obligations sneaking in. Fight against the urge to do chores and clean during this time. You can take a nap, put your feet up, read an uplifting book, or find something that brings you a feeling of relaxation. Spend time praying and thanking God during this time so your heart is also refreshed. Let your family know that this time of the week is reserved for you and do your best to protect it from things that want to creep up in your calendar. Your body is going through so much. You deserve extra rest.

Lord,

thank You for designing our bodies to need rest. Thank You for promising to give rest when we come to You weary and carrying a heavy burden. Provide refreshing strength to my body as I give it the rest it needs.

Amen.

Leading from Ahead

> Her mouth speaks wisdom,
> and loving instruction is on her tongue.
> PROVERBS 31:26 CSB

Proverbs 31 is a book of the Bible that teaches about a wife of noble character. King Solomon, the writer of Proverbs, lists various attributes of a virtuous woman. It can be intimidating to read through the list while comparing ourselves to her. Think of Proverbs 31 as a series of goals, but no one is ever going to live out each and every attribute perfectly. In verse 26, Solomon writes that "her mouth speaks wisdom, and loving instruction is on her tongue." As we personally grow to become more and more like Jesus, we can replicate what we've learned and teach it to our children. But we can't lead from a place where we haven't been ourselves.

We often have such lofty goals for our children in their spiritual and emotional development. While you're pregnant, you may have wondered if you'll birth the next great Billy Graham of the world. And who knows, perhaps you will! As mothers, of course we want our children to make a big impact in this world, but how will they if we don't teach them? And how can we teach from leagues behind them? In short, we can't. Leading is an action that is done from ahead. Would you follow a hiking guide through bear country if they had never hiked the trail before? Would you skydive with an instructor who had never ridden in a plane until the day you were supposed to jump?

If we are to have the "wisdom" and "loving instruction" that Solomon speaks about in a godly woman, we must discover who God truly is for ourselves before we can lead our children. Wherever we are in life, wherever we stand in our relationship with God, it's never too late to start following Him with our whole heart. Jesus is the best example we can follow, and He is a great teacher. Becoming more and more like Jesus is a daily choice. Each morning, we need to ask ourselves, "How can I follow Jesus *today*?" This way, we will be so much more capable of leading our children to follow Jesus too.

Jesus,
show me how I can follow after You today.
Teach me how to be a godly woman like in Proverbs 31.
You are my guide, and I am Your follower.
Thank You for being the greatest Teacher to ever live.
Amen.

An Attitude of Service

God has given each of you a gift from His great variety of spiritual gifts. Use them well to serve one another.
I PETER 4:10 NLT

Did you ever participate in a talent show while you were growing up? At your middle school talent show, in front of all your peers, it might have felt like you didn't measure up to the cool talents of the other kids. But you *are* incredibly gifted. Before you were even born, God knew you and who you were going to become. He gave you a "spiritual gift" that is unique and special. You can read about God's spiritual gifts in Romans 12:6–8; I Corinthians 12:6–10; Ephesians 4:11; and I Corinthians 12:28. Why does God give us each a spiritual gift?

Peter answers this question in I Peter 4:10, "Use them well to serve one another." There is a place or a project in which we are uniquely equipped to serve. When we are pregnant, it can be easy to take a break in serving our local church, our community, and our family. Of course, it's understandable that each of us needs to slow down a bit according to our physical symptoms, but don't fall into the temptation to use your pregnancy to get out of the gift of serving. God asks us to use the gifts He gave us to serve Him and to serve each other.

We are refreshed and encouraged by the action of serving, so don't deprive yourself of this encouragement in the months that you are pregnant. Find a space to volunteer that fits you and your spiritual gift. Maybe you are fantastic with young children, and you could serve in the children's ministry. Or perhaps you enjoy mentoring teenagers and could volunteer with the youth group. If you love to work with your hands, serve at a local food bank. There is so much you can learn about God just by serving others. It teaches you about the heart of God.

Lord,
show me what my spiritual gifts are
and how I can use them to serve You.
Help me to find the exact place and time
that I can serve others during the week.
Thank You for the gift of service.
Amen.

Living Out Our Mission

> For we are His workmanship,
> created in Christ Jesus for good works,
> which God prepared ahead of time for us to do.
> **EPHESIANS 2:10 CSB**

You were created for a specific purpose in this world. Think about it. God could have placed you in a different time period, in a different country, in a different family. But He chose here and now for your life. God put you on this earth for a reason, and each breath you take into your lungs is a gift and a reminder to live out your calling. Jesus tells us what our truest calling is in Matthew 22:37–39 (CSB): "Love the Lord your God with all your heart, with all your soul, and with all your mind. This is the greatest and most important command. The second is like it: Love your neighbor as yourself."

Love God. Love people. Those are our first marching orders.

But in Ephesians 2:10, Paul writes that we are "created in Christ Jesus for good works, which God prepared ahead of time for us to do." In addition to the two commandments that Jesus gave us, there are also specific actions that God has specially planned for us to accomplish in our lifetimes.

We have a mission and a purpose in this life. Some of us will have big callings like Mother Teresa, while others of us have callings that few people will ever notice. Both are equally vital to God's big plan for this world. In fact, you're already in the process of living out one of God's big purposes for you: motherhood. You are uniquely suited to this task, and discipling your children may be one of the "good works" that God has asked you to accomplish in your lifetime. When soldiers get an order for a mission, they spend time reviewing their objective, going over the plans again and again, and practicing the maneuvers they need to succeed. It's the same for us. How are you preparing for this mission that God has placed before you? Are you ready to step into this calling?

Jesus,

help me to discover what Your unique purpose is for my life. I want to be used by You to make an impact in our world. Help me to prepare for the mission of motherhood the best I can in the months ahead.

Amen.

Walking Authentically

*Don't let anyone think less of you
because you are young.
Be an example to all believers in what you say,
in the way you live, in your love,
your faith, and your purity.*
I TIMOTHY 4:12 NLT

Timothy is an important character in the New Testament. He became a Christian after hearing Paul preach during his first missionary journey, and he traveled with Paul for many of his other missionary journeys in the years after. We don't know much about Timothy other than what we find in Paul's various letters. Timothy had reservations and insecurities because of how much younger he was than fellow church leaders, but he continued the work that God set before him. Oftentimes, we can feel exactly like Timothy, inadequate and ill-equipped for what is coming. But Paul simply encourages Timothy to keep living out his faith authentically and with obedience.

Becoming more like Jesus is a personal choice and an individual walk. We don't need to compare ourselves with others. Instead, we can simply live our faith as authentically and genuinely as we can, no matter how inadequate we feel. Timothy became a leader of the early Christian church, and he was considered to be Paul's right-hand man and close friend. Though he had his insecurities, he walked forward with courage in spite of the barriers before him. In fact, he was martyred for his faith when he was trying to stand up for what he believed. Just like Timothy, we can leave our worries and insecurities behind and walk forward with courage and confidence. Timothy's story encourages us to each walk authentically in our faith as we follow in Jesus' footsteps. What are some ways that you can overcome insecurities about your faith in the weeks ahead?

Lord,
sometimes I don't feel prepared for what
You're calling me to do, especially motherhood.
But in spite of my insecurities, I know that I can walk
forward with genuine faith because You will be right there
with me. Teach me how to become more like You.

Amen.

Holding Tight to His Word

All Scripture is inspired by God and is profitable for teaching, for rebuking, for correcting, for training in righteousness, so that the man of God may be complete, equipped for every good work.
II TIMOTHY 3:16–17 CSB

Do you ever feel like you're praying at the ceiling and no one is answering? Do you ever wish that you could hear directly from God about what you're supposed to do in a given situation? Well, the truth is, we do get to hear directly from God on a daily basis! His Word is a letter to us. The Bible is a book of instructions, teachings, and encouragement that helps us figure out how to navigate this crazy life. Are there specific Scriptures for every single obstacle we might face? No. But there are so many verses that do apply directly to our lives and can encourage us as we become more like Jesus.

Pregnancy is a time when we can be at our very weakest, mentally, physically, and emotionally. It's a time when we can cling to the Bible for encouragement and strength even if we feel like no one is hearing our prayers. We don't have to be biblical scholars. We can simply read a passage of Scripture, pray, and ask God how we can apply it to our lives.

God will sometimes bring you to a passage of Scripture that is particularly applicable to what you're going through. Find specific passages that resonate with you and try to memorize them. When you're afraid or when you're having a particularly difficult day during your pregnancy, repeat these verses to yourself for encouragement and strength to continue on. God has given us an amazing tool for living. Set aside some time as often as you can to dig into the Bible and learn from what it says. Today, read Psalm 34, and take a few notes about what verses stuck out to you. How was it encouraging? How can you apply it to your day today and remember it when things get hard?

Lord,

thank You for the amazing gift of Your Word. I am so thankful to have access to Your written Word on a daily basis. Encourage and strengthen me through the Bible today.

Amen.

Washing Feet

> After washing their feet, He put on His robe again and sat down and asked, "Do you understand what I was doing? You call me 'Teacher' and 'Lord,' and you are right, because that's what I am. And since I, your Lord and Teacher, have washed your feet, you ought to wash each other's feet. I have given you an example to follow. Do as I have done to you."
>
> JOHN 13:12–15 NLT

The story of Jesus washing His disciples' feet is a very powerful picture of what He came to earth to do. He was the Son of God, the ultimate Ruler of the world, and yet He came humbly and quietly to accomplish His mission. The Jews thought the Messiah would come to conquer the Roman Empire and set up a new kingdom to rule. They thought there would be great battles and victories that would set them free from oppression. Instead, Jesus came as a humble carpenter and a traveling teacher. He turned their ideas about the Messiah upside down. Instead of conquering empires, He taught about loving your neighbor as yourself. Instead of setting up an earthly kingdom to rule, He taught that His kingdom is established in heaven and not on earth. Instead of freeing the Jews from oppression, He taught that His followers would face even greater persecution because of what they believed. He taught peace instead of war, love instead of hate, servanthood instead of conquering.

One of the greatest acts He performed to show this was washing His disciples' feet. As their leader and Rabbi, they should have been washing *His* feet. While customs today are quite different from the first century, there are still ways that we can "wash each other's feet" and show the same kind of love and humility that Jesus showed to His disciples. Are there other pregnant women or young moms in your life right now? What are ways you can step into their lives and serve them? Maybe it's volunteering to keep their children for a few hours while they get a pedicure. Maybe it's simply cooking a meal for another pregnant woman who is struggling. You have a clear insight into what they are going through. God might be giving you the opportunity to use your own struggles to encourage and strengthen someone else.

Jesus,

show me how You want me to wash others' feet today. Bring other women into my life who could use encouragement in their own journeys of pregnancy and motherhood. Use me to help others.

Amen.

Maintaining Obedience

But be doers of the word, and not hearers only, deceiving yourselves.
JAMES 1:22 ESV

When you buy your baby's crib, it will come with a set of instructions for putting the crib together. As you start building the crib, it's important that you read every step to ensure that you aren't missing something vital that could put your baby at risk. If you read through the instructions and then decide that your way is better, you could be misunderstanding what the manufacturer intended and put the crib together incorrectly.

Reading the Bible and then ignoring what it says is like reading the instruction manual for your crib and then deciding to build it your own way. The consequences of ignoring the crib's manual could potentially endanger your child. Ignoring the teachings of the Bible to live life your own way could endanger your soul and your spiritual well-being.

Of course, we cannot be doers of the Word if we don't read the Word first. Once we start holding tight to the Bible, we must take the next step and put its teaching into practice. Our walk of obedience is something we will work on for our entire lives. Some parts of the Bible are easy to obey. Other parts are harder. Obeying God is not always comfortable or easy, but it will ultimately enrich our lives when we choose to follow Christ, no matter what. If we want to teach our children to be godly men and women, we must show them what it looks like to obey God and His Word.

Next time you read a Scripture passage, pray and ask God what you can do to put it into practice. Pregnancy is a time when you desperately need God's strength. Maintaining obedience to His Word is important as you draw closer to Him.

Lord,
I want to be a doer of Your Word.
Teach me what it looks like to walk in
obedience each and every day.
Show me what You want me to do today.
Amen.

Surrendering Your Child

> We know that all things work together
> for the good of those who love God,
> who are called according to His purpose.
> ROMANS 8:28 CSB

Pregnancy is a season of surrender, even before the baby arrives. It's about surrendering our comfort, our control, and our circumstances for nine months. And then after, we will learn more about walking in surrender as a parent than we ever did before we got pregnant.

So what exactly does it mean to surrender our child to God? The first step is transparently asking ourselves if we really trust the Lord when it comes to our baby and our future children. God doesn't promise that bad things won't happen. In fact, we can be certain that trials will come for both us and our children. We cannot protect our children from every hurt that comes their way. The Bible does not promise an easy existence or the absence of pain. But it is telling us that whatever we face, whatever our children face, God can use all things for good in the end to fulfill His purposes. Can you trust that God has good for your child, regardless of what may come?

Once we can confidently trust God with our children, the second step is to relinquish the tight-fisted control and protection with which we want to cocoon our baby. The future is in God's hands, not ours. God Himself surrendered His only Son to a world of pain and condemnation. God understands what it feels like to be a parent watching their child experience suffering. He can empathize with us when we walk through trials or watch our children experience trials. The process of surrendering your child to God starts during pregnancy and will continue for their entire lives. God is in control, not us. But He does promise to be with us. He promises that, somehow, all things work together for good in the end, even if it's hard to see at that moment. God does want what is best for your child. You just have to trust Him.

Lord,
it's so hard to trust You with my baby's future.
It's so hard to walk in surrender when it comes to my child.
But I want to start trying to give my control and worries to You. You have good in store, no matter what.
Amen.

Surrendering Your Own Plans

> I have been crucified with Christ,
> and I no longer live, but Christ lives in me.
> The life I now live in the body, I live by faith in the
> Son of God, who loved me and gave Himself for me.
> **GALATIANS 2:20 CSB**

I wasn't sure I wanted kids after I got married. I was scared of babies and small children, and I enjoyed simply being married to my husband. We lived a pretty peaceful life, and I didn't want to see that disrupted or changed. In the end, God made the decision for us when I got pregnant with our son. My first thought was one of pure shock. And then, surprisingly, grief. I saw all those sweet, quiet evenings with my husband swirling down the drain. I looked into the future and witnessed my hopes and ambitions disappear with the reality of parenthood overshadowing all else. I felt panicked and completely out of control of my own life and future dreams.

God wanted me to realize that I'd been holding too tightly to my reality and what I thought my future would be. I was being very selfish to believe that everything would always stay the same and that my dreams should come before everything else. I'd forgotten what my ultimate calling was, and it wasn't "wife" or "manager" or "writer." It was "follower." It took getting pregnant to show me that I'd stopped surrendering my life and future to God. I was making my own plans and chasing after dreams that I'd never consulted God about. Galatians 2:20 can give us a simple reminder of our true calling: "I have been crucified with Christ, and I no longer live, but Christ lives in me."

You might have been like me, and your pregnancy was a bit of a surprise. You might feel like your own future is hazy and uncertain now that you have a child in the picture. God decided that *now* is the time for your future to change. It's your job to simply say, "okay." One day, you'll be so grateful that the future you had planned was replaced by the one where you get to live with your child or children.

God,

thank You for reminding me that my future plans are just vapor. My true calling is to be a follower of You. I give You control of my plans today.

Amen.

A Lesson from Hannah

Then Hannah prayed: "My heart rejoices in the LORD! The LORD has made me strong. Now I have an answer for my enemies; I rejoice because You rescued me. No one is holy like the LORD! There is no one besides You; there is no Rock like our God."

I SAMUEL 2:1–2 NLT

In the Bible, Hannah's story begins with her unable to get pregnant after years of trying. Other women made fun of her because of her inability to conceive. Hannah went to the Tabernacle of the Lord to beseech God for a son. During this time period, it would have been unusual for a woman to leave her husband to pray alone at the Tabernacle. In fact, the priest, Eli, thought she was intoxicated because of how she was praying. Hannah wasn't using the typical prayers from the Law. She was simply crying out to God in her own words and in her own heart. She promised God that if He would give her a son, she would dedicate him to lifelong service to God—and that she would take her young son to Eli the priest and leave him there to be raised in the temple. And God heard her.

So many women can relate to Hannah's anguish. Perhaps you spent years walking through infertility, praying and begging God to bless you with a child. Perhaps the child you're carrying right now is a miracle baby you never thought you'd have. Now, imagine following in Hannah's footsteps and dedicating that long-awaited baby into God's service. Hannah relinquished her own rights to raise her son, Samuel, and she knew that she would most likely never see him. Yet, she surrendered the child to God just as she promised after he was weaned. Imagine how difficult it must have been for her to walk away from that baby she'd waited so long for. But Hannah was a woman of integrity and faith. She put God first over her own desires, and then she did what she said she was going to do.

What a remarkable story of surrender and obedience that we can learn from today. Hannah understood the most important truth: Our children are ultimately God's, not ours. Then, in I Samuel 2:1–2, she sings a beautiful song of rejoicing to God for answering her prayer, a picture of devotion and love for God, her Provider.

Lord,

thank You for using Hannah's story to remind me that my baby is ultimately Yours.
Thank You for blessing me with this precious little life.
Help me to learn what surrender looks like.

Amen.

Miracle in the Making

A Lesson from Abraham

> Then Isaac spoke to his father Abraham and said, "My father." And he replied, "Here I am, my son." Isaac said, "The fire and the wood are here, but where is the lamb for the burnt offering?" Abraham answered, "God Himself will provide the lamb for the burnt offering, my son." Then the two of them walked on together.
> **GENESIS 22:7–8 CSB**

The story of Abraham and Isaac is one of the hardest Bible stories for parents. Abraham and his wife, Sarah, had waited and prayed for years to have a child. In their old age, God granted them a son, Isaac. When Isaac was a youth, God commanded Abraham to take his son up the mountain and offer him as a burnt offering. For many parents, our first thought is: *Why?* Why would God ask a parent to do such a horrendous thing? Surely that couldn't be His plan. God was testing Abraham's obedience and trust. He wanted Abraham to realize that Isaac wasn't his at all. He belonged to God. Abraham was prepared to be obedient to God's command. But he also fully believed that God would step in and provide what he needed.

Of course, at the end of the story, God does provide a ram for the burnt offering, sparing Abraham and Isaac in the process. In many ways, this story parallels what God was planning to do with His own Son millennia later, when Jesus came to earth to be the ultimate sacrifice. It's a foreshadowing of the pain that God the Father would experience as He watched His Son become the blood sacrifice for us.

What can we learn from this story? First, Abraham understood the fundamental truth that his son wasn't his. God created Isaac, and Abraham trusted that God would do what was best for his son in the end. Second, Abraham walked in obedience, even when God asked the impossible. He didn't back down. He surrendered his only son into God's hands. God isn't asking us to walk the same exact path as Abraham, but He is asking us to take a step back and remember who really holds our children in His hands.

Lord,

thank You for the story of Abraham and Isaac. You are the God of the universe, and You hold all things together. My baby is safe in Your hands, and I can trust that You will do what is ultimately best.

Amen.

God's Ways Are Not Our Ways

> "My thoughts are nothing like your thoughts," says the LORD. "And My ways are far beyond anything you could imagine. For just as the heavens are higher than the earth, so My ways are higher than your ways and My thoughts higher than your thoughts."
>
> ISAIAH 55:8–9 NLT

Walking in surrender to God is not an easy path, especially when things go wrong or bad things happen. We see it all the time. There are realities that many parents must face, like child autism, birth defects, rare diseases, developmental disorders, and the list goes on. It's okay to feel afraid when we think about some of these very real and difficult circumstances.

Loving and trusting God doesn't mean that everything will be perfect for us or for our child. Even when we surrender our baby's life into God's hands, hard things might still occur. It's so easy for us to *blame* God when the trials of life come and *forget* all about God when circumstances go our way. When the worst seems to occur, we lash out at God and ask, "How could You let this happen?" Perhaps, even in your pregnancy, you've received a test result or a screening that made you ask this question. God is strong enough for your questions, and He's compassionate enough to carry the burden of your anger, even if it's directed at Him.

We will never fully understand God's ways and purposes in this world. But the pain and grief are real. The questions are raw and vulnerable. How can God let such terrible things happen? Especially to such innocent, little creations like babies?

It's not our place to understand fully what God's purposes are. In Isaiah 55:9, God reminds us that "My ways are higher than your ways and My thoughts higher than your thoughts." There is purpose in the chaos and good even in suffering. We can question. We can grieve. But we can also trust. He is still in control.

God,

I don't understand why such terrible things happen.
I may feel angry. I may feel betrayed.
But Your thoughts are so much grander than mine.
I can't see the full picture. But I trust that You are in control and will be with me through it all.

Amen.

Surrendering Our Own Strength

My health may fail, and my spirit may grow weak,
but God remains the strength of my heart;
He is mine forever.
PSALM 73:26 NLT

God uses pregnancy to shape and mold us each differently. We will each face our own failings and weaknesses in a brand-new way during the weeks and months ahead. Some women who like to do things in their own strength will find themselves humbled. Our prideful natures can come out and tell us, *This is a chance to prove just how independent and strong you are. You are so much stronger than everyone else.* We should not compare our "strength" to others. Each woman carries strength within her for pregnancy, but ultimately, we can't do this without God's supernatural help. It's time to set aside pride and surrender our own strength. It's never going to be enough to see us through. We need God's presence each and every day. Perhaps He is using pregnancy to show you how much you've been relying on yourself. There is nothing that shines light on your weaknesses quite like pregnancy. It's a great opportunity to work on your own heart.

What have you been holding on to during these months? Do you struggle with pride or self-reliance? Take a few moments to ask God what He is trying to teach and reveal to you during pregnancy. Grab a journal or a sheet of paper and write down some thoughts about what you've learned about yourself so far and where you think God wants you to grow. It's hard to surrender your own strength, especially for those of us who are used to being on our own and relying on ourselves. But God doesn't want you to do this life alone. He wants you to rely on Him for what you need. There is nothing you need to prove. You're already so strong and brave. With God's help and support, you can walk through pregnancy and let God teach you about humility.

Lord God,

be the strength of my heart today. I admit that I cannot walk through pregnancy in my own power and strength. I do need You. My human strength just isn't enough. Thank You for growing me during this time.

Amen.

Surrendering the Past

Therefore, if anyone is in Christ, he is a new creation. The old has passed away; behold, the new has come.
II CORINTHIANS 5:17 ESV

Have you ever been to a bonfire or a campfire? When you got back home, you probably noticed that the smell of smoke and wood clung to your hair and your clothes. The scent of that bonfire lingered even after you'd left the scene. The past can feel like that. It can linger around you even when you feel like you've finally left it behind. And it will remain until you take a dramatic action, like a double-rinse cycle, to wash it away. While you've been pregnant, has the past crept back up on you? Perhaps you've been remembering some mistakes you made years ago. Perhaps you are dwelling on some bad things that happened to you. None of us is perfect. We all have things that haunt us from long ago. Let's not allow the past to control us in the present and negatively affect the future. Whatever you've done in your life, it's been forgiven. When Jesus died on the cross, He redeemed all the mistakes you've made: past, present, and future. You can start fresh today and walk into motherhood without the baggage you might feel like you're carrying.

When your baby comes, he or she is a brand-new creation in this world. That little life is starting fresh. Just like your baby is something totally new, you can also start fresh by embracing the redemption that God offers us. Since God can wipe away your sins, why would you choose to hold on to the painful past? Let today be a first step in self-forgiveness. You can surrender the past to God and move into a new season. Let this pregnancy be a marker of freedom in your life.

Jesus,
thank you for forgiving me of my sin—past, present, and future. Help me to leave the past behind and walk toward a future of freedom. I don't want to carry the baggage of yesterday into my tomorrow of being a mom.
Amen.

Praying for Your Baby's Faith

*"Truly I tell you," He said, "unless you turn and become like little children,
you will never enter the kingdom of heaven."*
MATTHEW 18:3 CSB

Pregnancy is a time of waiting and preparation. It can feel like you're in a plane, flying in a holding pattern for a long time, waiting for approval to finally land. But you can fill the months of pregnancy with productive action, and what is more productive than prayer? Prayer is a powerful tool that allows you to communicate to the God of the universe on behalf of yourself, others, and the world. Now is a great time to pray diligently for your baby's life and future. Grab a journal and jot down your prayers over the next few weeks. Someday you can look back at what you prayed for and see how God worked in your baby's life.

Today, spend some dedicated time praying specifically for your baby's faith journey in the future. As a mother, it can be easy to fret over the path that your children may take. Will they choose to follow the right path? Will they make bad choices? In the end, it is their decision, not yours. But you can do your part and begin to pray now that their hearts will be open to listening to the truth of God's Word and accepting what it says.

Dwight L. Moody, a prominent preacher and evangelist in the 1800s, stated, "It is a masterpiece of the devil to make us believe that children cannot understand religion. Would Christ have made a child the standard of faith if He had known that it was not capable of understanding His words?" Jesus told His disciples in Matthew 18:3 that they must "become like little children" to "enter the kingdom of heaven." Children can comprehend complex ideas in a simple, pure way. They love innocently and trust wholeheartedly. Pray today that your baby will come to know Jesus personally at a young age. Pray that he or she will have a strong faith for their entire lives and desire to share it with others.

Jesus,
I pray for my baby's faith today.
I pray that he or she will listen to what
the Bible says and grasp what it means for them.
I pray that my child will be a follower of You
all the days of his or her life.
Amen.

Praying for Your Baby's Birth

> The LORD is my strength and my song,
> and he has become my salvation; this is my God,
> and I will praise him, my father's God,
> and I will exalt him.
>
> **EXODUS 15:2 ESV**

It is natural to feel uneasy and nervous as you near your baby's due date. But you do not have to be afraid. God is with you, and He is not going to leave your side. As you spend dedicated time in prayer in the upcoming days and weeks, write down some of your specific fears about labor and share them with God. Acknowledge your apprehension and nervousness and then give them to God for safekeeping. Spending months fretting and anxious will not make labor less painful, but it will drag you down in the present. God designed your body to carry a baby and to deliver him or her. You can do this. Whatever happens, whether you're at the hospital or at home, God will be with you.

Exodus 15:2 says that "the LORD is my strength and my song, and he has become my salvation." Pray that God will be your strength on the day of your baby's birth. Pray that the labor and delivery will go smoothly with no complications. God is a God of detail. You can pray for the smallest things to the biggest requests. Pray that the baby will be head-down in the weeks leading up to delivery. Pray that the umbilical cord will stay away from the baby's neck and head. Pray that your body will stay strong and healthy and avoid complications like preeclampsia. If your birth plan includes a natural birth, pray for that! Or if you plan to have a C-section, pray that the procedure will go smoothly and that you will heal quickly. If you plan to give birth without medical pain relief, pray that God will give you the necessary pain tolerance and strength you need to accomplish this. In the end, the final outcome is up to God, but you can ask God to prepare the way for the birth that you hope for even as you trust Him with the birth that He has already planned.

God,

I give my baby's birth to You. I pray for a safe delivery and a healthy baby. I pray that You will help my body heal and recover after the baby is born. You are my strength and song. I can do this with Your help.

Amen.

Praying for Your Baby's Health

Dear friend, I hope all is well with you and that you are as healthy in body as you are strong in spirit.
III JOHN 1:2 NLT

As you walk through this time of dedicated prayer for your baby, take a few moments today to pray specifically for your baby's health. Sometimes people with good intentions can still terrify us with stories of birth defects, illness, or injuries from labor. But their stories are not your story. There are always potential outcomes that could happen, but worrying does nothing to keep them from happening. Jesus told His disciples in Matthew 6:34 (CSB), "Therefore don't worry about tomorrow, because tomorrow will worry about itself. Each day has enough trouble of its own." Instead of spending months worrying about what could go wrong with your baby's health, put your energy into specific prayers for their growth and development. If you haven't downloaded a pregnancy app yet that tracks your baby's development, find a good one that you like and check it each week. Use this as a tool to fuel your prayers. For example, you can start your prayer with thanksgiving: *Thank You that my baby's ears are developing this week.* And then follow it up with a specific prayer: *I pray for the healthy growth of my baby's hearing so they will be able to hear the Word of God and listen to the truth.*

When your mind travels to the worst-case scenarios, turn to prayer. Each week is a milestone of your baby's health and growth. They are getting bigger each day. Their organs are forming before your eyes. As you wait for test results and ultrasounds, cast your anxieties on the Lord and pray specifically for each and every test. As John prayed for his followers in III John 1:2, you can pray that your baby is "as healthy in body as [they] are strong in spirit." Update your journal each week with your prayers for your baby's development milestones. One day, when they open their eyes to look at you for the first time, you'll look back and remember the very week that you prayed for those beautiful eyes to develop.

I pray for my baby's health and growth today. You are in control of their development in the womb. I pray that my baby will be healthy, happy, and whole as they grow and change in the weeks ahead. Hold them in Your hand, God.

Amen.

Praying for Your Baby's Character

> . . . and that Christ may dwell in your hearts
> through faith. I pray that you, being rooted and
> firmly established in love, may be able to comprehend
> with all the saints what is the length and width,
> height and depth of God's love.
> EPHESIANS 3:17–18 CSB

This world can be hard on people. We see young teenagers make poor decisions and young adults walk away from their faith. Sometimes we can get so caught up in the ugliness of the world that we wonder if our children will be able to navigate it. But remember, it was also hard for the early Christian church. We can still do our part to teach our children about God and what He says through His Word. As this world continues to change, our children will face situations and circumstances that we never have. It's important to start praying now, even as he or she is growing in your tummy, for their personality and character. Read Scriptures to your baby as they are in the womb. Ephesians 3:14–21 is a beautiful prayer to read to your baby bump. Pray that your child will be "rooted and firmly established in love" and that he or she "may be able to comprehend . . . what is the length and width, height and depth of God's love." In the late second trimester, your baby's ears will develop to the point that they can listen to your voice and learn to recognize it! So as you pray for them, pray out loud so they can hear too.

Write down your prayers for your baby's character. For example, you can pray that your child will have a heart like King David and be a man or woman after God's own heart. Pray that they will be courageous and steadfast in the face of persecution and adversity. Pray that they will know and understand the truth of the Bible and stand for justice in our world. Pray that they will be someone who shows kindness to everyone and thinks of others before themselves. Pray that they will be passionate for the Gospel and desire to share God's story with others. Pray that they will be a doer of the Word and put their faith into practice. A mother's prayer is a strong and powerful force of nature.

Lord,
I pray today for my child's character and personality.
I pray that You will use them for good in this world.
Let my child be a man or woman after Your own heart.
Amen.

Miracle in the Making | 127

Praying for Your Baby's Childhood

*Train up a child in the way he should go;
even when he is old he will not depart from it.*
PROVERBS 22:6 ESV

It is amazing how much children can comprehend from an early age. Two-year-olds can start memorization and can remember lyrics to songs. By the time a child enters kindergarten, they understand right from wrong and show a guilty conscience when they don't obey. Parenting is probably on your mind a lot these days. While pregnancy is a time period of hard work, the job description of "mother" goes fully into effect after the baby comes. That is when the big challenges start.

It's time to start thinking about how you want to parent. What should discipline look like? How will you start teaching your children about the Bible from an early age? How will you conquer all these new responsibilities? You're not alone.

Most importantly, you should go to God for wisdom and direction. Spend time praying now for your baby's upcoming childhood. Write down your questions and fears and turn them into prayers. Search the Bible for guidance and wisdom about how to parent a young child, a preteen, and a teenager. Pray specifically for wisdom on where to send them to school. Should they go to public school? Private school? Be homeschooled? Pray for guidance on what to do for daycare if you work. Pray about all the medical decisions you'll need to make for your child along the way as they grow. It's never too early to start praying for the future. While you're waiting patiently for this new, sweet life to come into the world, prepare the way for their childhood through prayer. You won't be able to protect them from all the pain that comes from being human, but you can start praying for the Lord to give you the words you need to say to help your children navigate their lives.

Lord,

I pray today for my baby's childhood. I know time will fly by before I know it, and he or she will grow up so fast. Please give me wisdom on how to be a good parent and how to teach them about You and Your Word.

Amen.

Praying for Your Baby's Future Friend

*There are "friends" who destroy each other,
but a real friend sticks closer than a brother.*
PROVERBS 18:24 NLT

Think back on your childhood and your teenage years. Who were your friends? How did they affect you and impact your decisions? Were you blessed with friends who led you down good paths? Or were your friends constantly pulling you away from wise choices? How many of your bad decisions came from interactions with your peers and friends? Friendships are vital for humans in every stage of life. God created us to desire friendship. But sometimes, our relationships can become toxic and unhealthy. Friends can influence us positively and negatively. Your child's friendships can shape their future. So start praying now that your son or daughter will find uplifting, encouraging friends who are perfectly placed in your son or daughter's lives to bring about exactly what God has for your child.

Pray that God will bring other young families into your life right now who have children around the same age. Pray for a community of believers who can encourage you as a parent and offer lifelong friendships for your child. Embed yourself into a local church community where your child can go to a kids' ministry and learn about God and make friends. Pray that God will give you wisdom and discernment about whom your children should make friends with. And thank the Lord when He does provide those friendships for your children along the way.

Jesus,

I pray now for my baby to have strong, encouraging friendships through their childhood. I pray that You will provide a close-knit community that we can join who will walk alongside us through the entire journey ahead.

Amen.

Praying for Your Baby's Future Spouse

> This is why a man leaves his father and mother and
> bonds with his wife, and they become one flesh.
> **GENESIS 2:24 CSB**

Grab a few tissues and have them at the ready. We're going to jump forward in time a few decades. Someday, sooner than you can imagine, you'll be sitting in the stands, watching your baby walk across the stage at their high school or college graduation. You'll be moving them out of the house and into a place of their own. Your season as primary mentor, discipler, and teacher will be over, and they will be officially on their own in this world. Then, someday, they will meet someone special and fall in love. You'll meet this person and watch as your little child, the one who kept you up all night kicking in your tummy for all these months, will marry that special someone and start their own lives. Wow. It's hard to look that far into the future, but it will arrive sooner than you think!

Whatever your own experience has been with marriage, you can still hope and pray for the absolute best marriages and spouses for your children. You'll find the strength you need to be a good parent from developing a powerful prayer life in the years to come. Start right now.

Choosing whom to marry is one of the most important decisions your child will make in his or her life.

Pray specifically that your child will find someone who is wholeheartedly pursuing their faith. Pray that this person will be a courageous leader and a compassionate giver. Pray that he or she will be someone who will commit to a lifelong marriage with your child. And pray that their marriage will be strong and shielded from the attacks of the enemy.

Lord God,

I pray for my baby's future spouse. I pray that my child will find a godly man or woman who will encourage them in their faith and walk through this life side by side as one flesh. I pray that You will protect their future marriage from the enemy's attacks.

Amen.

Preparing Your Heart

*Guard your heart above all else,
for it determines the course of your life.*
PROVERBS 4:23 NLT

The forty weeks of pregnancy are all about preparation. And waiting. And then waiting a little more. But God designed pregnancy exactly the way He did for a reason. It's a true miracle that a woman is able to grow a new, precious life in her own body. Perhaps God made pregnancy last as long as it does to give mothers time to prepare for what awaits. Use this time productively. Work on yourself. Spend time with God to deepen your connection to Him. Look inside your own heart to root out anything that doesn't need to be there and ask for forgiveness. It's the perfect time in your life to start brand new when the baby comes.

Proverbs 4:23 states, "Guard your heart above all else, for it determines the course of your life." The Hebrew word for "guard" used here is *natsar*. It also can mean "to preserve" or "to watch over." Like farming, hearts require tilling and weeding so good things can grow. Before this precious, little baby joins your family, what needs to be pruned out of your heart? How can you use the weeks ahead to prepare the soil to grow the good things of God? The term "guarding your heart" is often used in terms of dating relationships. But the context of the original language shows that you are meant to preserve and watch over your heart and keep it from evil. Have you been preserving the goodness of your heart?

In Matthew 6:21 (CSB), Jesus says, "For where your treasure is, there your heart will be also." Have you stored up treasure in heaven, or have you invested your heart in the things of this world? Preparation requires steps of action. Dive deep into your own heart today and root out anything you might have been ignoring. Life will only get busier when the baby arrives. Use this waiting period to spend dedicated time with God, preparing your heart to be the best mother you can possibly be.

Dear Jesus,
search my heart and show me anything that doesn't need to be there. I want to spend time preparing my heart to be right before You. Help me walk into this next season of life redeemed and set free.
Amen.

Preparing a Special Place

> There is more than enough room in My Father's home. If this were not so, would I have told you that I am going to prepare a place for you? When everything is ready, I will come and get you, so that you will always be with Me where I am.
>
> JOHN 14:2–3 NLT

Preparing for the baby's arrival can bring about a mix of joy and apprehension. Many mothers experience "nesting" in the final weeks before the baby is born. You might have the urge to clean, organize, or redecorate the nursery over and over again. It's the instinct that God created in mothers to ensure that the baby has a special place prepared just for them. Getting the baby's room ready can be a fun activity to do with your family, or it could bring about new stress with all the decisions to make. What should the nursery theme be? Should you go with blue or green? What is the best brand of crib? Has the room been baby-proofed adequately? Sometimes the nursery decisions can be taken too far. The most important thing is that the baby has a special place prepared just for them when they arrive.

Taking steps to prepare your home for the new baby is a great reminder of what Jesus promises to do for us in heaven. Before He ascended into heaven, Jesus told His disciples that "I am going to prepare a place for you" (John 14:2). Even right now, Jesus is meticulously preparing a special place for eternity with your name on it. He is making decisions about your heavenly home just as you are making decisions about your baby's room. Your baby won't care what color the walls are or how expensive the furniture is. They will only care that they are near you, their mama, and that they are safe and loved. In the same way, when we get to heaven, we won't care about the size of our mansions or the length of the golden-paved sidewalks in front of our houses. We will only care that we are with Jesus, our Savior. So don't sweat the small stuff. Enjoy the preparation process while releasing the unnecessary stress of "nesting."

Jesus,

thank You for preparing a special place for me in heaven with You. Thank You for taking special care to make decisions about my heavenly home. Help me to create a sweet, special place for my baby here on earth.

Amen.

Preparing to Love

Love is patient, love is kind. Love does not envy, is not boastful, is not arrogant, is not rude, is not self-seeking, is not irritable, and does not keep a record of wrongs.
I CORINTHIANS 13:4–5 CSB

When I found out I was pregnant, I was worried that I might not be able to connect emotionally with our child. Babies and young children had always made me nervous, and for a time, I wasn't sure I wanted to have children. But God blessed us with a positive pregnancy test, and I had to confront my fears: Would I be able to love my child like he needed to be loved? It seems like a silly fear now when I look at him and hold him in my arms. Loving my son is the most certain thing in the world. The love of a parent for a child is perhaps the closest we will ever get on this earth to understanding God's love for us. If you have the same concerns that I had, rest easy. The maternal instincts will kick in. When you hold that baby, something will automatically click on inside of you. You'll fall in love with that little screaming bundle.

But love isn't always easy, even when it's your child. There will be days of endless screaming. There will be nights of pacing the house, humming and bouncing your baby and praying that he or she will fall asleep. There will be triumphs and heartbreaks throughout their childhood. It might not always be easy to love them, but you can start preparing your heart to love your baby right now while you're pregnant.

First Corinthians 13 is a well-known passage from the Bible that is mostly talked about in terms of marriage. But it can easily apply to loving your child as well. Paul writes, "Love . . . is not self-seeking, is not irritable, and does not keep a record of wrongs" (vv. 4–5). You might feel a little bitter toward the baby in your belly right now. You might be tired of pregnancy and all the aches and pains that go along with it. You might even hold the unborn baby responsible for your suffering. But loving your child starts now. Read the entire passage of I Corinthians 13:1–8 today and put that kind of love into practice.

Lord,

I need Your help to love my baby the way they need to be loved. Help me have the kind of love referenced in this Bible passage. Give me Your strength to selflessly love my baby no matter what.

Amen.

Preparing Financially

> But don't begin until you count the cost. For who would begin construction of a building without first calculating the cost to see if there is enough money to finish it?
> **LUKE 14:28 NLT**

Jesus challenged His disciples in Luke 14:28 to "count the cost" of becoming His disciple. He gives the relatable example of calculating the cost of constructing a building before starting the project to make sure there is adequate funding to finish it. In the same way, we are to consider the complete cost of following Jesus before we step forward in obedience. Just as the builder calculates the cost of a building project before beginning, it's time to start calculating the cost of a baby before the baby arrives. Whether the pregnancy is expected or not, preparing financially for a new baby can be nerve-racking and stress-inducing. But just like following Jesus is well worth the cost, sacrificing financially for a baby will be worth it too.

Take some time to pray about your finances. Ask God to give you and your family wisdom as you look over your income and budgets. Set aside time to sit down with your spouse and discuss how you can best prepare for the baby's arrival. There are great tools out there that you can use to set yourself up for success financially. You can take a budgeting class or download an app that helps you map out your potential expenses. Do some research on current diaper prices. Determine if you'll be using formula so you can anticipate those costs. Babies are expensive, but so many people in the world have children successfully. Regardless of how much money you make, you can do this.

God has shown up for my family in so many amazing ways financially. Turn to Him for guidance as you wrestle with any fears about how you will provide for your little one. You can trust God while also "counting the cost" of what the future will look like with another addition to your family. Take a few steps this week to set your mind at ease when it comes to your finances.

Dear Jesus,

please give me wisdom as I plan out how to provide for my baby's needs. Please show up in my life and show me how to budget my income in the best way possible. I trust that You will provide for our needs.

Amen.

Preparing Your Family

> Then God blessed them and said,
> "Be fruitful and multiply. Fill the earth and govern it.
> Reign over the fish in the sea, the birds in the sky,
> and all the animals that scurry along the ground."
> **GENESIS 1:28 NLT**

When God created Adam and Eve, He gave them a few very important jobs. In Genesis 1:28, God blesses Adam and Eve and tells them to "be fruitful and multiply." Children were to be a blessing to them when the world was perfect. God's original design was for Adam and Eve to have children and fill the earth with their descendants. Having children is a blessing, and we get to further the original call for Adam and Eve to fill the earth. As you begin to prepare your family for the baby's arrival, continue to remind yourself, your husband, and any other children you have that the new baby is a blessing.

If you're a first-time mom, the arrival of a new baby will be the ending of a chapter in your life. So soak up the sweet moments with those you're closest to, even if you are bursting with excitement over the baby's upcoming due date. Pray that you will remain strong and steadfast in the stressful newborn months ahead. Seek guidance and advice from other parents so you're as prepared as you can be.

The new baby is a gift and a blessing, but it will change the family dynamic. If you have other children, take time to make them feel special and loved as individuals, and talk often about the baby's arrival and how life might change. God chose your family to be the loving home for this little life inside of you. He chose you and your husband to be the baby's parents. He chose your other children to be big brothers or sisters. Spend some time this week preparing your family for the big changes and adventures ahead.

God,

thank You for choosing our family to be the loving arms that welcome this new baby. Prepare us each individually and as a family unit. Sustain our relationships and give us patience and strength.

Amen.

Preparing a Faith Foundation

*Therefore, everyone who hears these words
of Mine and acts on them will be like a wise man
who built his house on the rock.*
MATTHEW 7:24 CSB

Read the full parable in Matthew 7:24–27. Jesus tells a story about two men. The wise man built his house on a strong, secure foundation, and the foolish man built his house on the sand. When the rains came, the wise man's house stood firm while the foolish man's house fell with a crash. Jesus compared the wise man to someone who hears His words and puts them into practice, and the foolish man is someone who does not.

It's time to start building a strong foundation, both for you and for your growing family. Dig into the teachings of Jesus and ask God how you can put them into practice. If you want your baby to have a foundation of faith, show them how with your own example.

It's important that we prepare our children for the days ahead. When we have a strong foundation of faith, our house will stand up to the test of waves and rain. As a mother, you'll face new trials and times of testing, but following Jesus means that you've built up a foundation of trusting God and walking in obedience.

What's the main difference between the wise man and the foolish man from the story? Both of them heard the same teaching, but only one of them took action and put it into practice. Take steps of obedience after you read the Bible. Your baby will watch your own faith journey and learn from you. You will have a major impact on your child's faith story, and you can start now to create a strong faith foundation that will see your family through the times to come.

Jesus,

I want to be like the wise man who built his house on the rock. Show me how I can be obedient to Your Word today. Help me to build a strong foundation of faith for myself and for my children.

Amen.

A Lesson from Deborah

> Deborah, a prophetess and the wife of Lappidoth,
> was judging Israel at that time.
> JUDGES 4:4 CSB

If you think your life is busy now, just wait until you add a new baby to the mix. Juggling all the roles and responsibilities you carry as a mom can be difficult, but you can prepare yourself now for the new addition of being "mama" to everything else you do. One woman in the Bible demonstrated that balancing multiple responsibilities is possible.

It was very rare for a woman to operate in a leadership role in the Old Testament, but Deborah served as one of the judges of the nation of Israel. A judge at that time was a primary leader of the people. Israelites came from all around to seek Deborah's counsel. In Judges 4:4, it says that she was "a prophetess and the wife of Lappidoth." She had a very important job as a judge and a prophetess. She heard directly from God and spoke His words to the people. Deborah was also a woman of strength and independence. She even went with an army into battle. In Judges 5:7 (CSB), Deborah describes herself as "a mother in Israel." This is the only title she gives herself. She could have said that she was a judge or a prophetess. But in her song in Judges 5, she only refers to herself as a mother.

Deborah understood balance without forfeiting her individuality and strength. You can be a strong working mom, or you can be a strong stay-at-home mom. The central message to learn from Deborah is that she was obedient to what God called her to do. She is one of the few women mentioned by name in the Old Testament, which shows just how important she was to the people of Israel. Deborah was a leader of leaders, a warrior of courage, and a woman who was proud to wear the title of mother. As you look into the new reality ahead, remember that you *can* balance all the titles that you will carry. Whether you're an executive, a cashier, or a stay-at-home mom, you can bring glory to God through your work and through your obedience. If Deborah could carry all the responsibilities that she did while being an amazing mother, you can too.

Lord,
help me to learn from Deborah's example.
Help me to balance all of life's responsibilities
as I look forward to being a mom. Help me to glorify
You through my work and by being a mother.
Amen.

The Miracle of Pregnancy

*I will praise You because I have been
remarkably and wondrously made.
Your works are wondrous, and I know this very well.*
PSALM 139:14 CSB

Creating new life inside of your womb is a miracle that only God could perfect. Your growing baby began as just a tiny embryo. By the middle of week three, the baby's heart develops and will beat approximately 54 million times before birth.[1] The amniotic sac offers a protective home for the baby throughout the pregnancy, and the amniotic fluid facilitates lung development and offers nutrients in the later stages. By week twenty, the baby can hear and respond to sounds outside of the womb. From here, your child can start to listen and learn to recognize the sound of your voice.[2]

By twenty-six weeks, their eyes can produce tears. Their highly developed eyes will have over 100 million light-sensing cells called rods.[3] Over 100 million! Isn't that amazing? And each of these tiny cells was formed and put into perfect place by God's design. By the end of

---

[1] "Prenatal Form and Function—the Making of an Earth Suit." 3 to 4 Weeks | Prenatal Overview, The Endowment for Human Development, https://www.ehd.org/dev_article_intro.php.
[2] 4 to 5 Months (16 to 20 Weeks) | Prenatal Overview, The Endowment for Human Development, https://www.ehd.org/dev_article_intro.php.
[3] 6 to 7 Months (24 to 28 Weeks) | Prenatal Overview, The Endowment for Human Development, https://www.ehd.org/dev_article_intro.php.

pregnancy, the baby's brain will have almost 100 billion fully functioning neurons.[4] The entire process of labor and delivery is an incredible showing of God's great attention to detail.

Psalm 139:14 states that we have each "been remarkably and wondrously made." There are countless amazing facts about the baby's development in utero. An absolute miracle is occurring right now inside your body. During the times of discomfort and fatigue in the days ahead, take a moment to thank God for developing such an amazing process to bring new life into the world. The miracle of pregnancy and birth should remind us of God's existence and His incredible power. Nothing is possible without God's design. He crafted your body to nourish and protect your baby for around forty weeks. Each cell of your baby's body is coming into being from the safety of your tummy. That is an incredible honor and privilege as a mommy. Only you will ever truly experience what it's like to grow this unique and beautiful life. Isn't God amazing?

God,

thank You for choosing me to experience this incredible miracle. I pray that You will continue to grow and develop my baby in the weeks ahead. You are truly an amazing Creator.

Amen.

---

[4] 9 Months to Birth (36 Weeks to Birth) | Prenatal Overview, The Endowment for Human Development, https://www.ehd.org/dev_article_intro.php.

Miracle in the Making

Making Disciples

Therefore, go and make disciples of all the nations, baptizing them in the name of the Father and the Son and the Holy Spirit. Teach these new disciples to obey all the commands I have given you. And be sure of this: I am with you always, even to the end of the age.
MATTHEW 28:19–20 NLT

Jesus gave the Great Commission to His followers right before He ascended into heaven. It was His final command and promise to His friends, and it is still true for us today. We are told to make disciples of all nations. For some people, obeying this command looks like moving overseas to be full-time missionaries. For others, it might include becoming a vocational minister. For many, it looks like sharing their faith with coworkers, neighbors, and friends. The call to motherhood comes hand in hand with the call to make disciples. As a mother, you are automatically a disciple-maker. Most likely, you'll be the first person to share Jesus with your child. You'll be the first voice they hear read the Bible to them. And perhaps you'll be the person who gets to sit with them as they accept Christ into their hearts.

You don't have to move overseas or quit your job to be obedient to the Great Commission. Being a parent grants you an incredible opportunity to make disciples under your own roof. In verse 20, Jesus tells us to "teach these new disciples to obey all the commands I have given you." Making disciples goes further than just sharing your faith. It's a process of teaching and leading and modeling what it looks like to be a follower of Jesus. Your children will follow the example that you set for them. Prepare your heart now to be the best model possible for your baby. Draw close to Jesus so you can share your experiences with your family. He promises that He will be "with you always, even to the end of the age." What a special role you will have as a mother and a disciple-maker. It's a high calling and responsibility.

Jesus,

I pray that my children will come to know You personally. Help me to show them how to follow Your ways and walk in Your love. Teach me how to be a great disciple-maker.

Amen.

What It Means to Be Mama

Her children rise up and call her blessed;
her husband also, and he praises her.
PROVERBS 31:28 ESV

Pregnancy is the first step on the pathway to motherhood. You're already a mama right now. When you finish the pregnancy journey and hold your baby, it's simply another step on the long road of being a mom. Being a mama is an amazing gift from God. It comes with major responsibilities, times of stress, many sleepless nights, and changes to your body that will stick with you for a long time. But it also comes with adorable smiles, baby giggles, first steps, and years of making new memories. It means leaving behind an old version of yourself and fully embracing the best name you'll ever have: Mama.

Closing chapters in our lives is never easy. Change never is. Whether you're going from two kids to three or from no kids to being a mom for the first time, nothing will ever be the same. It's normal to feel apprehensive about the unknown future and what new reality a baby will bring to the picture. But there are precious moments when it's just you and your new child—when you look down at them and feel your heart expand with more love than you ever thought it could hold. There's the certainty in your heart that you would do absolutely anything for that baby. No matter what. It's the kind of love that only a parent can understand. And you know what? It's modeled straight after God's love for you.

Wearing the team jersey of "mama" is a special privilege. Some women will never experience it, but God chose you to bear the title. Being a mama means you are no longer focused on yourself. You will learn what true selflessness looks like, and you're already learning how to be selfless through pregnancy. No mom is perfect. You will make mistakes. Your family isn't going to be flawless. There will be times when you want to run away from it all. But God called you to motherhood. Your children may never fully understand what you sacrificed for them, but that doesn't make your sacrifice less meaningful in their lives. So take heart, Mama. You were made for this.

Lord,

thank You for calling me to the role of mama. Help me to live in such a way that my children will want to call me blessed. Give me the strength to love my children the way You love me.

Amen.

The Role of Caretaker

*So let's not get tired of doing what is good.
At just the right time we will reap
a harvest of blessing if we don't give up.*
GALATIANS 6:9 NLT

According to the Merriam-Webster dictionary, a "caretaker" is "one that gives physical or emotional care and support." What isn't mentioned is that the role of caretaker is a 24/7, 365-day-a-year responsibility when you're a mother. There are no company holidays or summer breaks for parents. As a caretaker, you're on the clock all the time, and that can become very draining over the long haul.

Caretaking means taking care of someone who can't care for themselves. It's one-sided at the beginning. You'll give and give and give to your child without receiving anything in return. Pregnancy is the start of this giving relationship, and it won't change until your child is older. On the days right now when you feel tired and uncomfortable, remember that you're already stepping into your role of caretaker for the baby inside of you. You're taking care of a little life who can't take care of themselves. It's a heavy responsibility.

Galatians 6:9 tells us not to "get tired of doing what is good." There will be times during pregnancy and even more times after the baby comes that you will feel like giving up. But caretaking for your child is a good thing. They need their mama. They need a caretaker. God chose you for that role. Paul continues on to say that "we will reap a harvest of blessing if we don't give up." There is no bigger blessing than watching your baby gaze up at you and smile. You don't have to step into the role of caretaker in your own strength. Ask God to provide what you need to be the best mother you can be.

Ruth Bell Graham said, "As a mother, my job is to take care of the possible and trust God with the impossible." You don't have to be a miracle worker. You just need to show up for your children day in and day out, and trust God for the strength to continue on. With God, all things are possible.

Lord,

I pray that You will teach me how to be a wonderful caretaker to my children. Show me how to keep giving even when I'm tired and weary. My baby is a blessing from You. Thank You.

Amen.

A Lifelong Commitment

> Most important of all, continue to show deep love for
> each other, for love covers a multitude of sins.
> **I PETER 4:8 NLT**

The call to motherhood comes with a lengthy timeline: the rest of your life. It's a real commitment. It's for life. Think about the last wedding you attended. You probably watched the happy couple speak vows to each other, promising to commit to each other "as long as they both shall live." Unfortunately, many times, that happy couple's promises will be broken when divorce occurs. But when you have a child, there's no ceremony or witnesses documenting your vows to your child. You won't make promises in front of an officiant. And unlike marriage, you can't divorce your children. They are yours for better or worse. You're committed in a permanent way that even marriage can't touch.

If this is a bit heavy to you, you're not alone. Becoming a parent is a weighty burden, but it comes with so much joy and fulfillment. In many ways, you're speaking marriage vows to your baby right now, even when he or she is in the womb. You're promising to nurture and care for them from this day forward, for better or for worse, for richer or for poorer, in sickness and in health, as long as you live on this earth. No matter what, you'll be their mommy. No matter how old they get. No matter where they go in life. They are yours.

No one else in this entire world will get to experience what you will be for your children. Motherhood is a high calling. It's a big responsibility, and it requires a huge commitment, endless patience, and great perseverance. But you don't have to do it alone. Look around you for a support network. It may include your husband, your parents, friends, or your church community. While no one will ever be able to take over your role as mother, you can surround yourself with helpers. As you look into the future, do so with confidence and excitement. Motherhood is a high calling, but God chose you for a reason. Your baby needs *you* to be their mama.

God,

give me the strength to be the best mother I can be for the long-term commitment of parenting. Show me those whom You've placed in my life who can be a support to me.

Amen.

Miracle in the Making | 157

For Such a Time As This

> If you keep silent at this time, relief and deliverance
> will come to the Jewish people from another place,
> but you and your father's family will be destroyed.
> Who knows, perhaps you have come to your
> royal position for such a time as this.
> **ESTHER 4:14 CSB**

The story of Queen Esther in the Bible reads like a fairy tale at first. A peasant girl becomes queen of an empire. When her people are threatened, Esther steps forward and risks her life to beseech the king to spare the Jews. God orchestrated her rise to power "for such a time as this" (Esther 4:14). He specifically placed her as queen at that time and place in order to protect His people and execute His will. Sometimes we can only see God's hand at work after the fact. When Esther was chosen to be queen, she could have never guessed that the purpose for her queenship was to stand up for her people and save thousands of lives. God is always at work, and it's amazing how we can look back on our lives and see His plans unfolding.

Just like Esther was chosen to be queen, God has specifically chosen you to be a mother to your baby "for such a time as this." If you were waiting patiently for years for that positive pregnancy test or you were a bit surprised, it was all in God's perfect timing. He chose you. He has called you forth into a new stage of life: motherhood. God has decided that right now is the time for you to step into this new role, whether you're going to be a mommy for the first time or are adding a new baby to a growing family. Esther was afraid of stepping out in obedience to God's calling, but she did it. It's okay to feel intimidated by this calling in your life, but God chose you for a reason to be the mommy to your particular, uniquely created baby. He has decided that right now is the right time to call you up to the big leagues. Why? Because God has put you right where you are, right when you are, and made you *who* you are for such a time as this.

Lord,
thank You for choosing me right now
to be a mother to the precious, new baby in my tummy.
I trust Your timing and Your plan.
Show me how we fit into Your plans and purposes.
Amen.

LIVE YOUR FAITH

Dear Friend,

This book was prayerfully crafted with you, the reader, in mind. Every word, every sentence, every page was thoughtfully written, designed, and packaged to encourage you—right where you are this very moment. At DaySpring, our vision is to see every person experience the life-changing message of God's love. So, as we worked through rough drafts, design changes, edits, and details, we prayed for you to deeply experience His unfailing love, indescribable peace, and pure joy. It is our sincere hope that through these Truth-filled pages your heart will be blessed, knowing that God cares about you—your desires and disappointments, your challenges and dreams.

He knows. He cares. He loves you unconditionally.

BLESSINGS!
THE DAYSPRING BOOK TEAM

Additional copies of this book and
other DaySpring titles can be purchased
at fine retailers everywhere.
Order online at <u>dayspring.com</u>
or
by phone at 1-877-751-4347